IF JESUS HAD A DOG

BY
DONALD H. HART

PRESS

Preface

GOD

Saint Anselm said, "God is that which no greater can be thought of." That, of course, has always been the problem for me concerning God. I cannot fathom an infinite universe when I look up at the stars at night without my head exploding, much less think about a *Being* that created it all. So God has always been a *thing* to me, not a real being. Then along came Jesus. God knew humans needed Jesus so we could see him, touch him, feel him, love with him, hurt with him and learn from him. Jesus was absolutely a historical figure that lived two thousand years ago. But whether you believe in the divinity of Jesus is a matter of personal faith. Franz Werfel wrote in his novel, *The Song of Bernadette*: "For those who have faith, no explanation is necessary. For those without faith, no explanation is possible." It's your choice to believe or not, it's always been that way.

DOG

For me there is *no* life without my four-legged canine friends. Without them I would simply be a walking corpse. My parents loved me and I loved them, but that love always came with conditions. Husbands, wives, children all love one another BUT there are plenty of conditions attached to that love. Of all the dogs I have had come in and out of my life, there have *never* been any conditions attached. It has always been pure, unconditional love. The ancient Greek's called it Agape love. I impose certain conditions on my dogs—they never impose any on me. They seek only to serve and love. This must be how God's love is toward us-pure, unconditional love. I don't think I could or would want to live a life without one. This is how deep my love for dogs is—perhaps you are the same!

GOD/DOG

To me it is no coincidence that dog spelled backward spells god and god spelled backward is dog. God gave us "man's best friend" to show us how *He* loves us, just as a dog does. So for me I say, <u>for those who have known the love of a dog, no explanation is necessary. For those without this love, no explanation</u>

is possible. This book is simply a bridge to get the reader to the other side and show the humanity of Jesus in a new light. Hopefully during your journey this work will help strip away some of the religious dogma surrounding Jesus. What better way to present you Jesus and his life, his ministry and his message than with his "best friend"—his dog.

HOW TO READ THIS BOOK

Scripture quoted is from the World English Bible and the New International Version.

Words that are in regular type are from me, the author.

Words italicized in bold are words of Jesus taken directly from scripture.

Words in regular type bold are words I have given to Jesus.

This book is very different because of the subject matter. You will constantly be shifting gears on each page-going from what the author writes, to what the Bible says, to what Jesus says, back to what the author writes. At first it seems a little daunting, but you'll soon find it's a fun way to read a story as it keeps your mind engaged, constantly shifting those mental gears.

*D*edicated to: All the four-legged friends that have shared my life with me. Thanks for the love and the thousands of walks and talks we've had together.

An angel of the Lord came to me in a dream and said, "Tell this story". The following is that story...

Now the birth of Jesus Christ was like this; for after his mother, Mary, was engaged to Joseph, before they came together, she was found pregnant by the Holy Spirit. Joseph, her husband, being a righteous man, and not willing to make her a public example, intended to put her away secretly. But when he thought about these things, behold, an angel of the Lord appeared to him in a dream, saying, "Joseph, son of David, don't be afraid to take to yourself Mary, your wife, for that which is conceived in her is of the Holy Spirit. She shall bring forth a son. You shall call his name Jesus, for it is he who shall save his people from their sins." (Matthew 1:18-21)

Chapter 1

Joseph Weds Mary

About fifteen miles southwest of the Sea of Galilee and seventy miles north of Jerusalem lay the small, peasant hamlet of Nazareth. Few people in the ancient world ever would have known of Nazareth, nor would have cared about it, until this story was told. There were only about two hundred families in this place and within one of them was a man named Joseph, a descendent of the priestly line of Levi, one of the twelve sons of patriarch Jacob. He was in his early twenties and worked hard at his trade as a carpenter. He was no different than the other young men in the village who were looking to make their mark in life and start a family.

There was also a young girl in the village named Mary, who had caught the eye of the young carpenter. She had just turned sixteen and was now considered of age to marry. There weren't many young women in a small place like Nazareth, and Joseph had had his eye on Mary since she was twelve. When she became of age, he asked her father if he could court her. Her father, also a descendent of Levi, gave his blessing and their courtship began. Like millions of young couples before and since, they went for long walks together and talked of their future. Joseph loved her more and more with each passing day. He loved her long, flowing black hair, which moved effortlessly in the wind. She had a soft voice to match her soft, olive skin. He liked that she was no stranger to hard work—she was always seen helping her family. She was rather tall for a Jewish girl, but certainly not taller than him. She had large brown eyes and a wholesome, radiant smile that made Joseph feel warm all over. They would often talk about having children and having their own home someday. They were a young couple deeply in love.

One day during one of their walks, Joseph and Mary sat in the cool shade under a large oak tree. While gazing into her dark brown eyes, he carefully took her baby-smooth hand, placed it in his rough, calloused one and asked if she would marry him. "Yes," Mary said, without hesitation. She had fallen for the carpenter even before he had asked her father if he could court her. She liked his work ethic, his charming personality and his sense of humor. Mary felt fortunate, for many of the marriages in her day were prearranged at birth, but she was going to marry a man she loved! They kissed each other for the first time. Even the wind seemed to agree to the union as it raced through the leafy boughs of the mighty oak, making whispering sounds.

However, as Mary was busy planning her wedding, something very shocking and perplexing occurred. She was alone one evening in her small room where she lived with her parents. An angel of God visited Mary and informed her she would soon be pregnant with a child. Mary was quite startled that someone, or something, would suddenly be in her room. The angel was Gabriel; he told her not to be afraid, that she would bear a son, who would be called Joshua (Hebrew: "Yahweh Saves," Greek: "Jesus"). He would be great, would be called the Son of the Highest and would be given the throne of his father, David. He would reign over the house of Jacob and his kingdom would have no end.

Startled, Mary had one question: *"How can this be, seeing I am a virgin?"*

The angel answered, *"The Holy Spirit will come on you and the power of the Most High will overshadow you. Therefore also the holy one who is born from you will be called the Son of God."*

Gabriel waited for Mary's reply, for it was not imposed on her to do this. God gave her the choice to be part of this or not. Mary, being of pure heart and spirit, said to Gabriel, *"Behold, the handmaid of the Lord; be it to me according to your word."*

Since the time of Isaiah's prophecy some seven hundred years earlier, that a virgin Israelite would bear a son who would be the Messiah, many young virgins in Israel who had heard of God's promise were hoping they would be so blessed as to fulfill that prophecy. Mary was overwhelmed that this signal blessing had been given to her! The angel left her just as suddenly as he had appeared. She immediately collapsed and fell asleep—the encounter had drained her of all her energy.

The next day when she awoke, she had memories of the encounter with the angel but felt it must have been a dream. She went on with her day and tried to put it out of her mind—it was simply too overwhelming to think about.

Mary had just learned that her older cousin Elizabeth was six months pregnant with a child. She had an overwhelming compulsion to go visit her cousin and informed Joseph of her plans. At this point she didn't think she could share with him the seemingly fantastic story about an angel visiting her. She felt she needed someone to talk to who could make sense of the angel's visit and whether it even really happened. (Elizabeth's husband, Zachariah, a Temple priest, had also been visited by the angel Gabriel, who told him that she, his wife, would have a son although she was past childbearing age.) Since Mary didn't tell Joseph why she wanted to go, he certainly did not understand the reason for such a quick and unforeseen visit. However, since the betrothal period usually lasted a year before a wedding took place, he gave his blessing on her trip. This would allow him more time to concentrate on providing for their future.

Mary left Nazareth the next day. When she arrived, Elizabeth greeted her excitedly—she said that even the child in her womb kicked for joy when he heard Mary's voice! Mary settled in to help out for the next three months, which delighted Elizabeth—having a child in old age was very tiring. Mary thoroughly enjoyed her time there. She could speak freely to Elizabeth about the encounter she had had with Gabriel—the older lady's husband had shared with his wife about the visit with the same angel. Also, Mary found that she was pregnant and confided this to Elizabeth. Up until then, she hadn't told another living soul! She and Elizabeth laughed often; it was such a time of freedom for Mary and it was a joy for her cousin to have such a guest! When Elizabeth's baby was born, he was named Johanan (Hebrew: "Yahweh-favored," "John" in Greek). History would come to know him as John the Baptizer.

After Elizabeth delivered her child, Mary returned to Nazareth with a very serious problem. By then, it was obvious to all that Mary was pregnant and Joseph was particularly devastated. The woman he loved was now carrying another man's child! That's all he could think about. Mary's father blamed Joseph and accused him of having relations with his daughter before they were married. Joseph, of course, knew better—he had never touched her that way! Joseph blamed Mary that she had been with a man while away for those months helping Elizabeth.

How could Mary explain this to Joseph? No one would believe her story; she knew she was pregnant and why—the angel had told her that, but she had never thought about how she could explain her situation to others, particularly to her parents and to her beloved Joseph. She hadn't thought about these consequences when she so readily agreed to the angel's proposition. She knew she was with child and she had never been with a man. How could God do this to her? Now she thought her entire life would be ruined.

For several months now she knew that the encounter with the angel was real—hadn't she and Elizabeth gone over this again and again? Finally, Mary cried her heart out to Joseph and told him all the details of the angel Gabriel's visit, but her story was just too unfathomable; he could not believe her! Joseph refused to be made to look like a fool! However, he still loved her and didn't want her to be harmed, so he planned to secretly call off the wedding.

That evening while Joseph was sleeping, an angel of God appeared to him in a dream, saying, *"Joseph, son of David, don't be afraid to take to yourself Mary, your wife, for that which is conceived in her is of the Holy Spirit. She shall bring forth a son. You shall call his name Jesus, for it is he who shall save his people from their sins."*

Joseph was tremendously relieved! How could he have even doubted his dear, precious Mary? Three days later, to the relief of Mary's parents, Joseph married Mary. However, her lifelong dream of a large village wedding now had been shattered. Mary had become the laughing stock of the villagers of Nazareth. Anyone caught in sexual relations before marriage was, according to the Law of Moses, to be punished—death by stoning! It had become dangerous for Mary to even go to the community well for water—people would turn their backs on her, whisper to one another about her, or threaten to take her before the Jewish authorities. Things became so hostile she quit going out in public.

Joseph, now knowing the truth, was furious the townspeople would treat Mary as they did. Several times he would accompany her to the well, seemingly daring anyone to say or do something to Mary. They never did. Joseph was tall and lean and no person in the village dared get on his wrong side. But they certainly had no problem talking behind his back.

Joseph could sense that the best thing he and Mary could do was to relocate elsewhere. It was evident the ignorant villagers of Nazareth would always be talking about Mary and her "state".

During this time a decree came from Caesar Augustus of Rome that all families had to return to their birthplace to be counted in a census for tax purposes; therefore it was decided Joseph and Mary should wed before the census. Without village fanfare they had a small family wedding. Since both Joseph's and Mary's families were of the house of David, whose home had been Bethlehem, they had to return there for the enrollment.

Joseph and Mary quietly said farewell to their friends and family. Joseph loaded a cart he had built with his own hands; he took with him the tools he used for his carpentry business. Mary asked why he was taking them and his only reply was, "Just in case they will be needed." Joseph knew they would not be returning to Nazareth, but he had no idea where they would call home. He didn't want to bother Mary with these thoughts in her "state", and they began the arduous journey to Bethlehem. They slowly made their way over the rough and rocky road, resting often as it was Mary's time to deliver her baby.

Now it happened in those days, that a decree went out from Caesar Augustus that all the world should be enrolled. This was the first enrollment made when Quirinius was governor of Syria. All went to enroll themselves, everyone to his own city. Joseph also went up from Galilee, out of the city of Nazareth, into Judea, to the city of David, which is called Bethlehem, because he was of the house and family of David; to enroll himself with Mary, who was pledged to be married to him as wife, being pregnant. (Luke 2:1-5)

Chapter 2

The Two Births

T he small cave with fencing around it served as a stable for many of the local animals. It was located a ten-minute walk from the inn where Joseph had lastly tried to obtain a room for the evening. Unfortunately, there was no room at that inn or any- where else. The town was filled with people who had come there to obey Caesar's census order. The inn- keeper and his wife regretted that they hadn't room for the couple; they could see Mary might deliver a baby at any time. The best the innkeeper could do was to offer them an overnight stay in their stable. It wasn't much, but at least it would keep them from having to spend the night outdoors. Joseph thanked the man and hurried toward the stable.

The stable had never seen such activity. At the time Joseph and Mary arrived, it was busy with the comings and goings of those who had checked in at the inn before them. These people (and even the animals) had no idea what a miraculous, world-changing event was to take place that night. Had they known, they no doubt would have stood tall and straight and in a state of joy at what was about to occur.

While the front of the stable was full of activity for a while, no one noticed that in the dark and inhospitable back of the cave something curious was taking place. A female dog was about to give birth. The dog had no name, no home, and no human to care for her. She was a homeless stray. Life for her, as it was for most dogs in the ancient world, was a day-to-day crusade of existence, searching for food, avoiding disputes or harm and seeking a safe place to sleep at night.

Born in the rolling hills surrounding Jericho some three years earlier, the dog led the uneventful life of a stray. The fact that she had even reached the age of three was somewhat of a miracle. Several times she had escaped death and it was simply by favor of her wit and instinct that she had dodged those do-or-die situations.

The female dog had no idea what compelled her to strike out on her own and make the overland trip to Bethlehem from Jericho. She had strong instincts and had followed them many times before, but this was different. This was like an actual physical force that seemed to guide her: first to the south and then to the west. She had but one goal now — to reach the town of Bethlehem in time. The reason for this newfound instinct escaped her, but it was intense and seemed to grow stronger with each step she took. It was as if her body received more energy with each mile she traveled on her journey. Finally, and with little physical strength left, she reached her destination, the small town of Bethlehem. She found herself on the edge of the town and walked down a cobbled path that extended past a dozen stone homes.

One of the homes had a large, domed window with two loaves of leavened bread perched on the ledge. Directly below the window, on the ground, lay a large piece of the bread. The hungry dog devoured it with haste and slid her tongue over her lips as far as it would reach for any crumbs that might be left. While walking the streets, she discovered an oversized rock with a large notch that was partially filled with rainwater. She stopped and lapped it all up. She then followed her nose, which led her to the stable full of various kinds of animals. This is where she thought she could safely spend the night. She quickly slid under a railing toward the back of the stable into the dark part of the cave. She was certain no one had seen her, not even the animals.

Near the back of the cave was a pile of straw that was dry and warm. As she lay down to rest, the impulsive feeling that had been brewing within her was released. She knew she had reached her journey's end.

As she shifted the straw to fit the contour of her shape, her eyes adjusted to the darkness. She noticed she was in the company of several camels, donkeys and sheep. As her eyes examined the place, she looked for any openings that would provide a quick exit if needed. Just then a cart pulled by a donkey eased to a stop just outside one of the two entrances. The noise of it disturbed some of the animals and the donkeys began to bray. They quieted down as they saw a man and woman, neither of whom appeared to pose a threat. The man quickly made his way to the back of the cart and turned to assist the woman lying in the back.

He immediately began to gather dry straw and prepare an area that would provide them rest and comfort throughout the night. He left the woman alone and returned to the innkeeper seeking help, as he could see the woman's time was near. The female dog felt sadness as she realized she had never had anyone to love her and care for her like the man was doing for the woman. As she closed her eyes, she thought how nice it would be to be part of a human family. She dreamed of this as she fell peacefully asleep.

Later that evening, the dog suddenly awoke — an amber glow had enveloped the cave and filled it with warmth and light. She wrinkled her nose as she sniffed for the smell of fire and then thought it to be peculiar, as there was no sign of fire at all. The light was intense, but it was not searing like the rays of the sun. It was soothing and seemed to bestow a sense of peace and tranquility throughout the little cave. She noticed that the man had left the cave and that the woman was talking to someone, and yet, she was the only visible human in the cave. Was the woman talking to herself? she thought.

Suddenly, instincts kicked in and she recognized it was time to give birth, just as thousands of generations of dogs before her. Now her thoughts were not of a loving home, or an empty stomach, or all the activity that was occurring in the other part of the cave. Her sole focus centered on her ability to give birth to her new offspring. She thought she was going to have to do this alone, without help from anyone. Then, she noticed an object near the ceiling in her corner of the cave. It was translucent; she recognized an outline similar to that of a human, clothed in a beautiful flowing garment of pink, blue and violet hues. The object seemed to have feathered wings stretched wide, like a hawk she had once seen swoop down on a rabbit in the desert. The light-being brought her comfort and she wagged her tail as if to show relief that she would not be alone after all.

During the birth, the dog knew she would be fine—nature had prepared her for this moment. Two hours of exertion resulted in the birth of six puppies. Almost immediately they were searching for milk and contending for the best place to line up and receive their first feeding. Feeding her pups would be a problem. She was so weak from the journey to Bethlehem that she had only a modest amount of milk for the hungry pups. The light-being descended from the ceiling and lay down next to the young mother, gently stroking her forehead with the tip of its wing while feeding the starving mother manna from heaven. This was the same manna God fed the starving Israelites during the time of Moses. This instantly created energy and invigorated the mother so she could nourish her newborns.

At the same time the dog was birthing her litter, the woman in the front part of the cave was also enduring the labors of childbirth. She appeared to be the beneficiary of aid and comfort being offered by two figures. The figures appeared to be humans, but she could tell, even from a distance, they were not human. They resembled the light-being that was helping the mother dog, these beings were opaque; but they had the same wing like extensions. The dog used her nose, as smell is a canine's most important sense, to try to determine the nature of these beings. She wiggled her nose and breathed in and out in rapid succession, but they had no scent! She tilted her head in confusion—she had never encountered anything that did not have a scent about it! How could this be? she thought. She could see these beings were focused on the well-being of the woman as she labored and then delivered a child. Just like the hands of a clock gathered in passing each other in time, so were the two mothers as they gave birth within minutes of each other that night.

The two beings that had helped Mary with the delivery had departed before Joseph returned with the innkeeper's wife, Sarah. Joseph was amazed to see his wife holding a newborn baby boy, delivered just minutes earlier. Joseph's heart pounded loudly and he was so excited he had to remind himself to breathe. Joseph had entered into this marriage by faith. He believed that Mary's baby was of God having heard of her visit from Gabriel and experienced in his own visit by an angel. No one in Nazareth thought Mary was anything more than a promiscuous young girl. Joseph had once witnessed the stoning of a girl who was charged with lewd acts and immorality. He shuddered whenever he recalled the hostile and revolting images and stinging words that were cast upon the poor girl before she was stoned to death. So when Joseph first saw mother and baby together, he grew anxious. Although this was their first son, the child was not from him. He thought that he would have to work through this with himself and God. Joseph accepted the child as a gift of faith and, seeing the infant for the first time, paternal pride washed over him.

From the back corner of the cave Joseph heard some peculiar noises. He immediately recognized the sounds as those of small dogs, mostly newborn puppies. He didn't give any real thought to the stirrings, as his attention was focused on Mary and their newborn child. They named the baby "Jesus" just as Gabriel had instructed Mary before the conception.

Joseph was quite surprised as several shepherds from the surrounding hills came to pay homage to the newborn child. They didn't have much to offer in terms of gifts, as they were but poor, humble guardians of sheep. Joseph was taken aback as they knelt before Jesus, singing praises. Angels, they said, had directed them to the baby's birthplace.

While this was happening, Joseph caught the movement of something out of the corner of his eye. It appeared to be moving from the dark end of the cave. Again, Joseph turned his attention to the shepherds, Mary and Jesus. But the sound of something slowly making its way through the straw seized Joseph's attention and he realized as it drew closer it was, indeed, a newborn dog. How could this be? he thought. Joseph didn't know much about dogs. They were usually owned by the rich or shepherds. One thing he did know, however, was that it would be quite impossible for a pup just born to be moving far with its own efforts. Joseph noticed that this little one did not even have its eyes open, yet somehow it made its way, barely crawling on its belly, to the feet of Mary. Once it got that far, the helpless creature collapsed and fell asleep. It was completely exhausted from its journey of nearly fifty feet. Joseph carefully picked up the little dog and carried it back to its mother and litter mates. Before he left, he made sure the puppy was placed where it could get a good feeding of milk.

The shepherds, of course, knew much about dogs. Their very survival depended on their dogs. To them, this was a sign, that a newborn dog with its eyes still closed and struggling with all of its young might could make the journey over to Mary. For Joseph it was merely another strange thing that he had seen on this journey. Then one of the humble shepherds lay his staff at the feet of Jesus as an offering. Next to a good dog, nothing was more important to a shepherd than his staff. Legend had it that this was the same staff carried by Moses and had mystical powers. It was a mystery how it fell into the hands of these humble shepherds. Jesus would be seen his entire adult life walking the Galilean countryside with this same staff. Jesus, the shepherds said, would be the shepherd of men and would need this staff.

In front of the cave were some of the people from the crowded town who were coming and going. An unusual being, much like the light-beings, sat down on a boulder and played a harp. The harp appeared to be solid gold. Mary and Joseph had rarely heard this instrument before as it was usually only played for royalty or at the Temple. Everyone in the area was from humble backgrounds, so it was rare to ever hear the tones from a harp. Their ears perked up as this one was played; they had never heard pitches and tones such as this. Each vibration from the strings seemed to flow together, like the drops of water in a river, to make a melody that-like the river-had continuous movement and purpose. The effect was hypnotic and the mood in the stable, even among the animals, was one of perfect peace and harmony. Such an atmosphere of peace as this had not been felt since Adam and Eve were one with God in the Garden of Eden.

As the evening wore on, Mary had become quite exhausted from the trip, the birth and all the activity that had descended upon the stable that night. She felt special and honored at the wondrous events, but she was extremely tired. She swaddled the infant Jesus in a soft cotton cloth and lay down on her bed of straw. Joseph, some angels and the shepherds were keeping watch over mother and baby. But no sooner had Mary closed her eyes, than Joseph once again saw the little dog moving one clumsy leg after another toward Mary and Jesus. Joseph was perplexed and wondered how a dog could be birthed and begin walking within hours. As the newborn made its way to Mary and Jesus, Joseph noticed the little dog's opened eyes. Joseph marveled that the little hand-sized puppy had made its way over to them again! The infant Jesus was snuggled under Mary's arm and the pup nudged his way between Mary's hand and Jesus and then purposely shifted himself closest to Jesus. Now, everyone took this as a sign, but they didn't understand its meaning.

Once again upon reaching its destination, the puppy closed its eyes and immediately fell asleep, exhausted from the journey. Joseph again picked up the helpless creature and took it back to its mother. Although she was weary, she had noticed one of her brood was missing and she raised her head as if to say thank you for its return.

For it was decided by God that this little dog, not God himself, nor the angels and archangels of the universe, would be the protector of Jesus on Earth. His name would be Shomer ("protector" in Hebrew). This message was given to Joseph that evening by one of the angels present and then Joseph began to understand more clearly the spectacular efforts of the helpless creature.

Now when they had departed, behold, an angel of the Lord appeared to Joseph in a dream, saying, "Arise and take the young child and his mother, and flee into Egypt, and stay there until I tell you, for Herod will seek the young child to destroy him." He arose and took the young child and his mother by night, and departed into Egypt, and was there until the death of Herod; that it might be fulfilled which was spoken by the Lord through the prophet, saying, "Out of Egypt I called my son." (Matthew 2:13-15)

Chapter 3

Escape to Egypt

T he couple spent the next week in a room provided by the owner of the inn and the stable. Sarah, the innkeeper's wife, had told him of everything she had seen and heard that recent fateful night when a baby was born. The awed innkeeper decided not to tempt God, and he went out of the way to provide a room for the young couple.

When they moved from the stable, Joseph, though delighted with Mary's son, did not forget the other newborns left behind. Twice daily he made trips back to the stable to check on the mother dog and her puppies. Although all six from the litter looked pretty much the same, Shomer was the only one with eyes wide open and able to walk. The rest were helpless little newborns. Joseph knew it was important the puppies should be nourished well from their mother, so he brought scraps from the inn's kitchen to feed her. Joseph named the mother dog "Yalal" (Hebrew: "howl"), for she would often let out a mournful howl. Poor dog, he thought, she probably had many events in her life that were mournfully sad. She seemed to appreciate the daily visits from Joseph—someone actually cared for her! In her gratitude, she wagged her tail incessantly to thank him for his kindness on each of his visits. He was taking joy in overseeing the growth of the young family.

Joseph had the cart they brought from Nazareth, which held all of their meager possessions. As it turned out, their most valuable possessions were his carpentry tools. They found the citizens of Bethlehem to be so hospitable they decided to settle there permanently (they were determined not to go back to Nazareth!). Joseph soon found plenty of work and Mary quickly made friends with the local women. The innkeeper had taken on the care of Yalal and her pups. As soon as word got around in Bethlehem about the unusual birth of a baby in the stable, they also heard about the dog that gave birth there. There were plenty of offers to take one of the five as pets. Of course, Joseph kept Shomer, who took to his new home with delight. Shomer's favorite place was to be near Jesus—early on he seemed to realize he was the baby's guardian.

Eight days after Jesus was born, he was circumcised and later taken to the Temple in Jerusalem to be dedicated according to Jewish law. Things went well for the young family and it looked as if Bethlehem was a good choice for their future. The innkeeper helped them find a house and they settled in. Joseph was quick to let Bethlehem's citizens know his carpentry abilities and it wasn't long before his business was thriving. The shepherds who had come to worship the baby at his birth now became the family's friends. They would visit their home to check on him and when Jesus became a toddler, Joseph and Mary would take him and Shomer on short walks to the countryside to see their shepherd friends. Since both Joseph's and Mary's forebears came from Bethlehem, they were familiar with the stories of many of the shepherds, including King David. As they walked out to the fields, they could visualize the young David sitting on a rock and writing some of his many psalms.

Both Jesus and Shomer enjoyed their time with the shepherds more than anything else. Every season sheepshearing time came around. Many people came to shear the animals and there was plenty of food and it was a wonderful festive atmosphere. Shomer was a favorite of the sheep, he was so good to them, and Jesus loved playing with the little lambs.

The shepherds loved Shomer and taught him skills he would use all his life. In turn, the experience gave him a love for all shepherds. The young dog had no idea at that time the young toddler beside him would become known as the greatest Shepherd the world would ever know.

But as pleasant as their sojourn was in Bethlehem, events were unfolding that would soon change their circumstances. Almost two years after Jesus's birth, some Wise Men from Babylon arrived in Jerusalem and asked to see King Herod. They inquired of him as to where they could find the new king who had been born. Perplexed, the king called his prophets, who told him a Messiah would be born in Bethlehem. Herod sent the visitors on their way, requesting that they notify him if they found the child. The Wise Men did make their way to Bethlehem, found the house of the young boy Jesus, worshipped him and left him many gifts, including gold. But they were warned by God not to go back to Herod and left for home by another route. When Herod heard of this, he issued a decree calling for the death of any boy in Bethlehem under two years old.

It didn't take long for the citizens of Bethlehem to hear of Herod's decree and they had good reason to be afraid. Joseph knew that the king was probably looking for Mary's child, since he had so miraculously been born there. He quickly loaded their possessions, including his carpenter tools, and put Mary, Jesus and Shomer in their cart.

Before they left, Joseph left a gold piece from the Magi with the kind innkeeper to provide for the stray dog, Yalal. In turn he got the man's word she would be cared for and never want for food or a home. So in a strange twist of fate, the only thing the stray dog wanted in life was the love of a human family and she found it in the form of the innkeeper and his wife.

Joseph wasted little time in getting his family out of the reach of the insane Herod. That night, under cover of darkness, Joseph, Mary, Jesus and Shomer headed south to Egypt, a journey of some three hundred miles. Joseph made arrangements to rendezvous with a Macedonian trade caravan that was heading to that destination. Making the journey with a large caravan such as this one was of great benefit—it would provide protection from thieves and slave merchants and any number of other dangers on the long trip; besides, the leaders of the caravan knew the way. Instead of paying for passage as most had done, Joseph bartered for the passage. Joseph's end of the bargain was to be available for repairs to wagons, carts, wheels, cages and just about anything else that would require the expertise of a carpenter. This, however, proved to be much, much more work than Joseph had planned. There were around two hundred people in this caravan and there was no end to the breakdowns—especially cart wheels. Joseph had the cart they had brought from Nazareth loaded with their meager possessions, which included his most valuable ones—his carpentry tools.

On day three of the journey one of the men in the caravan that had a wooden leg came to see Joseph. After years of use, his wooden peg had finally splintered in half. This was very rare in the ancient world—most people who lost a limb died from the accident or from infection later on. The man was a retired soldier in the Roman army and had lost his leg in a battle near Carthage some ten years earlier. Over the years he somehow had managed to walk a lot of miles on that sturdy piece of wood. Joseph didn't feel as though he could help the man—he had never done a repair like that. To him, the leg of a table or chair was a quite different repair than the leg of a man! However, he told the soldier he'd keep an eye open for the right kind of wood—something not too dense and heavy to lift and walk, but strong, light and durable to abuse. As luck would have it, the next day they were traveling on part of the route that parallels the Mediterranean Sea for several miles. Along the way, Joseph stumbled on a piece of driftwood. Probably from a shipwreck, he guessed, and it wasn't too heavy or light. He proceeded to carve out a new leg for the soldier and, after numerous fittings, Joseph finally got it right. The man used the new leg the remainder of his life; he was always thankful for the carpenter Joseph for giving him the chance to walk again.

One kind of barter Joseph undertook was doing work for an animal broker. An animal broker went from region to region selling domestic animals to local people. At that period in human history, there were pockets of people that had never seen a camel, a goat, a cow, a sheep, etc. So the broker would pull into a village or camp and show the people how they could benefit by having some of his animals. Every so often they would obtain wild animals such as leopards, lions, bears, cheetahs and the like, which they would take to Rome for use in the Coliseum's gladiator shows. Repairing the animal broker's cages was basically a full-time job, but in return for all of

Joseph's work, the man provided plenty of food for the family—especially young Shomer.

At this point Shomer was just another mouth to feed and a burden to Joseph. However, Joseph could see that whenever the two-year-old Jesus and Shomer were together, it brought both of them lots of fun. Besides, Joseph kept remembering the command of the angel, which was to "take the dog with you as he is to protect the child all his days."

The trip was uneventful for Mary, Jesus and Shomer. What a wonder for Mary to watch the baby who was growing, who would become a man—who would become God! Did he see as a human or as a god? Mary queried to herself. She would stare for endless hours into the blue eyes of her little boy and wonder what mission God had for her and Jesus. She hoped that God would reveal this to her, but it was all right if he didn't. Her mission, she thought, was to raise the child according to Jewish tradition and she was going to do this with all her might.

Shomer, on the other hand, was turning out to be quite the handful for Mary. Shomer was now, at the age of over two years, fully grown—although he would fill out his large frame in the next couple of years. This amazed Mary as she had never been around a dog in her entire life. He loved walking beside the young boy and it was Shomer that taught Jesus to walk. Mary would prop Jesus up and Shomer would come next to Jesus. Jesus then hung onto the bushy coat of Shomer and they would walk together. Then, after a walking session, Jesus would lie down for his daily nap and Shomer would cuddle up beside him. Most of the time, however, he was as active as a busy bee and often under Mary's feet. One day she became exasperated and let the dog "have it." This was his first scolding and he didn't quite know how to react so he let out a yelp, moved away a few feet and dozed off to sleep.

After many (it would take more than three) weeks on the hot and dusty trail, the family arrived in Egypt without too much fanfare. Joseph was informed of a small Jewish community several miles south of Alexandria they called Hepru. Without haste, Joseph made their way to the little village. There Joseph and Mary settled down to live their new lives together until God would call them back to Israel.

They would live in Hepru for the next few years. This was a small hamlet of a couple hundred people. Most of the workers there supported the Egyptian royalty with their trades. Not all Jews had left Egypt some thousand years earlier with Moses. Joseph soon found a small house for his family. It was only one room, but it was large and had a solid roof. A new door was a priority—the old one fell apart when they first looked at the house. That was the first project for Joseph—the house had a perfectly strong and snug door by the end of the day. Mary was so happy she had Joseph for a husband; she could see such strength in him, but he also had a tender side. For example, his second project was to build a bed for Jesus. Jesus loved to be rocked to sleep, so Joseph decided to put rockers instead of legs for his bed. His greatest challenge was finding green wood he could bend for the rocker arms. After a long day searching the banks of the Nile, he found a stand of willows. The wood from this tree was well known for being pliable and Joseph knew immediately he could bend this wood to make rockers for his little boy.

One day Mary was sitting by the Nile while watching Jesus and Shomer play along the bank. She began to muse over Jesus's first word. It wasn't mother, it wasn't father—it was "Sho." Not Shomer, but Sho. Just as clear as day she had heard Jesus call his name. But no one ever called him Sho before. So from that day on, within the family, Shomer became Sho. He already knew his name and always paid keen attention when Mary or Joseph called him, but now his best friend called him Sho and he liked the sound of it coming from Jesus. It was a nice, short name and more direct to the point, he thought. Then, given his new nickname, he went and licked Jesus's face!

These early years of Jesus's life were fairly uneventful; he was simply busy growing up and being a little boy. However, Joseph and Mary were astounded at the inquisitive nature of the young fellow. It didn't matter—he seemed to want to know everything and anything about the natural world: bugs, clouds, the night sky, trees, birds and on and on!

In contrast, Shomer's early life was very eventful, for Shomer was learning how to become a dog. Most of the things he was learning came naturally—it was instinctive. Shomer was not given heavenly powers, but he was born with an awesome instinct and physical ability that went well beyond that of other dogs. This feature alone seemed to give Shomer magical powers that many would argue about over the years—wondering if he was some sort of four-legged angel. No, he was just a dog! He quickly learned how to use the sense of smell to his advantage. The first smell he ever recalled was the infant Jesus. Shomer was drawn to Jesus's smell from across the stable where they were both born. Even with eyes yet to open, he could maneuver from one side of the cave to the other by his sense of smell. Now that he was fully grown, he could raise his nose in the air and tell the difference between various animals just by smell. He could sense, just by smell, if a human intended harm to his family or not. He didn't even need his eyes to be in control of his world. He could smell fresh water a mile away and Jesus came to rely on him many, many times over the years to find drinking water on their journeys.

His sense of sight had become like that of an eagle. Once he was out hunting rabbits for his dinner and saw one in the distance—perhaps two hundred yards away. A human could never do that from that distance, but Shomer zoomed right in on it. Shomer had delicious rabbit meat for dinner that evening! He would often hunt alone. Not overnight outings, mind you, as he always had to come back to his home in the evening to protect his family—most especially the young Jesus. His sense of hearing was akin to that of a deer, only much more acute. He could hear a twig being stepped upon a hundred yards away. Many times his sense of hearing helped rescue him and Jesus from a bad situation. The cheetah is known as the fastest animal on land, but when measured for strength and speed, Shomer was the fastest animal in the world. He could reach a top speed of thirty five miles an hour in seconds and run down any creature.

Shomer was a force unequaled in the civilized world and quickly gained a reputation for his amazing feats. No person ever messed with Jesus physically until the end and lived to tell of it. But still Shomer would go out of his way to play with lambs whenever he encountered them as he never lost his gentle side.

Jesus loved to play with Shomer. He would tug on his ears to the point of pain, but the patient dog would simply roll over and Jesus would come after him for another round. Shomer loved the attention. Joseph didn't seem to have time for such things. And Mary was always too busy with taking care of Joseph and Jesus and domestic duties for such play. But Jesus loved it. One of Jesus's favorite things to do when he was very small was to ride the back of Shomer like a horse. Shomer had seen people on the backs of horses before, so he figured it was a cool thing for Jesus to do. But Shomer was a muscular dog, now weighing about one hundred pounds. Enough weight to be forceful, but not too much to slow him down. He had a long, bushy tail to balance him and very long legs, which gave him a long and fast stride. His color was black with a white spot on his chest. The spot looked very similar to the star that shone above the stable where he and Jesus were born. Jesus did confirm this years later when he was combing Sho's assumed the crocs had eaten them. Joseph and Mary were the guests of honor and much of the attention was focused on them. As people gathered around the open area next to the water to dance, sing and tell stories, the couple was briefly distracted and left Jesus and Sho alone for a moment. Sho lay down in the cool grass and took a brief nap next to Jesus. A yellow butterfly landed on Sho's side and this caught Jesus's eye. He tried in vain to catch the flying leaf in his little hands, but was unsuccessful.

No sooner had the couple turned their backs on Jesus than he fell into the croc-infested water of the Nile, chasing the butterfly. Immediately the river's swift current took Jesus some ten yards downstream. Jesus yelled out in panic, as he could not swim. Everyone turned around at the same time to see the boy being swept downriver and shouted out in disbelief. Crocs in the river were already at work and fighting one another to be the first at the feast. Within seconds Jesus was surrounded by three mighty Nile crocs. They could dismember a horse within a minute and the boy was nothing more than a small morsel, but a morsel they each coveted.

Everyone turned instantly to the sound of Jesus screaming. Sho instantly rose from his nap, surveyed the situation, took a running start and leapt some twenty feet in the air, landing on the back of one of the crocs. Using the leathery back of the croc as a platform, he ran towards its head. This croc was too focused on his next meal to feel anything on his back. To Sho's right was the young Jesus choking on water with the two other crocs rapidly moving fast in on their target. Just as they opened their mouths, Sho grabbed Jesus with his powerful jaws and snatched him out of the water. The crocs snapped down hard into nothing but air and it caused them to shatter many of their teeth. In the same instant Sho turned around, ran down the back of the croc and launched toward the bank. He fell two feet short of land, but the crocs were so stunned with what had just happened they could not recover in time. Sho pulled himself and Jesus out of the Nile onto the grassy bank and the people thought they had just witnessed a miracle of God. It wasn't. It was just Sho being Sho. Mary and Joseph wept as they got their little boy back and gave Sho the hug of his life. His tail could not keep still as he was so excited that he had saved the life of Jesus. Little did he know, but this wouldn't be the last time, and the legend of Sho was born.

*But when Herod was dead, behold, an angel of the Lord
appeared in a dream to Joseph in Egypt, saying, "Arise
and take the young child and his mother, and go into the
land of Israel, for those who sought the young child's life
are dead." He arose and took the young child and his
mother, and came into the land of Israel. But when he heard
that Archelaus was reigning over Judea in the place of his
father, Herod, he was afraid to go there. Being warned in
a dream, he withdrew into the region of Galilee, and came
and lived in a city called Nazareth, that it might be fulfilled
which was spoken through the prophets: "He will be called
a Nazarene." (Matthew 2:19-23)*

Chapter 4

Escape from Egypt

S oon after the rescue of Jesus by Sho on the Nile, as they were preparing to leave Egypt, the following happened. For centuries the Egyptians had been in love with their dogs. No civilization in the ancient world was so enamored with dogs than the ancient Egyptians. The Egyptians, however, had developed a special breed of dog that became known as the Pharaoh dog. This was the dog that a dead Pharaoh would take with him into the afterlife and they were held in high esteem throughout the land. Over the years, over the centuries, this dog came to exhibit some exceptional hunting skills through selective breeding.

The Pharaoh dog was light, yet strong. They were very nimble on their feet and could reach amazing speeds to run down most any game. They also possessed keen eyesight and could spot a hare one hundred yards in the distance and because of the pointed shape of their ears, they had exceptional hearing. As an all-around breed for hunting, none could rival the Pharaoh dog.

Every year since the time of Ramses, the Pharaohs would hold a race for the Pharaoh dogs. This was a special race to determine the absolute "best of the best" in the entire land. Great honor would be bestowed upon the owner. The winner and his dog would be awarded a position within the royal court of the Pharaohs and a prize of two talents of gold. This would be enough gold to support a small village for years. The last of the Pharaohs ended with the suicide of Cleopatra a few years earlier; now the leader of the land was a Roman general. The tradition of the race was still kept intact by the aristocracy and the race continued on an annual basis. The race consisted of ten dogs. These were selected to be the best in the land as judged by the top breeders in Egypt of Pharaoh dogs. No other type of dog had ever been entered, as the race was designed to capitalize on the strengths of the Pharaoh dogs. Simply put, other breeds would never stand a chance at winning the race. Additionally there was an entry fee of fifty pieces of gold. This entry fee meant the average Egyptian could never afford to enter. This was a race for the rich and privileged in the land. Joseph, while far from rich, still had some gold left over as gifts from the Magi years earlier and he decided to enter the race.

Sho, at the age of five, was now in his absolute prime and Joseph knew it. He filled out his large frame with steel-like muscles; he had perfected his hunting skills to rival those of the fiercest of African predators. He was fast and strong and most importantly smart—he had no rival in the land. So Joseph decided to take the risk and entered Sho into the race. He knew the Pharaoh dogs were very fast, but he had seen Sho run down a gazelle on one occasion so how, he thought, could any dog be faster? Sho was the last of the ten allowed to compete. Sho was the first of his kind to ever enter this race and was laughed at by the large crowds at the start of the race. Mary, Joseph, Jesus and supporters from their village were in the crowd, however their cheers were far outnumbered by the local Egyptians.

The race lasted two days with a grueling regimen of races and obstacles designed to clearly find out who really was the "best of the best" in all the land.

The first test started at the base of the Great Pyramid. Imagine Joseph, the young Jesus and Sho standing at the base of the Great Pyramid of Giza. Here was mankind's greatest marvel guarded by the Sphinx, looking out over Egypt—and beyond. Each of the ten dogs was outfitted with a special harness that fit around their necks and backside. Attached to the harness were two leads that attached to an Egyptian war chariot. Over the centuries the Egyptians had perfected the chariot and it was considered the ultimate war machine of its day, perfectly suited for desert battles. The chariot was usually powered by two horses. For this race, the power would be the dog.

Sho looked around at the other dogs in the race and let out a mild growl. He was slightly insulted that these "dogs," groomed so perfectly for this event, could even be considered to be at his level. They of course felt the same about Sho. How could a mutt like this even be allowed in this race? each dog thought to itself. The event was staged so that each dog would pull the heavy chariot through the sand as far as it could before stopping, usually collapsing in pure exhaustion. This race was designed to test strength-one dog pulling a chariot that normally took the power of two horses.

With all ten contestants aligned, their owners were now ahead of them by several yards to encourage their entrant. What a sight with Joseph and the young Jesus standing in front of Sho, offering encouragement. Sho didn't need any. He was going to make it a point to dominate the other nine. Then, without warning, someone off to the side blasted a trumpet and the race was under way.

Sho decided he would let the others jump out of the gate first and size up the competition. He looked to his left, then his right. Immediately to his right was a dominating Pharaoh in size. Most of the others were around fifty pounds, lightweights Sho thought, built for speed—not strength. But the one next to him, on his left, was a huge Pharaoh, weighing in around ninety pounds. This one, Sho believed, would be his greatest competition. The huge Pharaoh jumped to a large lead, coming in second was a Pharaoh Sho judged to be around seventy pounds and very strong. The rest were rapidly falling back and Sho could see they would not be in contention for this leg of the race.

With Joseph and Jesus running after Sho offering encouragement, shouting at the top of their lungs, Sho took control of the race. He rapidly passed the other seven, including three that had stopped dead in their tracks from exhaustion. Pulling a four hundred pound chariot through the sand was no easy task, even for two horses. Sho put on a burst of speed and he blazed through the Egyptian desert, his long muscular legs digging into the sand with each stride. He was easily breathing through his muzzle, not even opening his mouth. Suddenly, as he closed to within twenty feet of the second-place dog, it stopped and collapsed. Sho shot past him and zeroed in on the big Pharaoh, the one he knew would be his greatest competition. Now neck and neck with the giant Pharaoh, they both looked at one another, each wondering how long the other could keep this pace. Their hearts were pounding through their chests and their muscles were getting weak. They were now over a mile from the start—a record. But Sho could see his competition was rapidly nearing exhaustion. His tongue was dangling and white foam was gushing from his mouth. The Egyptian sun was burning down upon both of them. Even Sho's rear leg muscles were quivering from the strain of the pull. But Sho was not going to give in. Then, a few seconds later the giant Pharaoh collapsed, near death from the ordeal. Sho gave the giant dog a slight recognition, but then knew the race was over.

At that point Sho had won the race, but he decided he was not done. He made a large turn of the chariot and began to pull it back to the start of the race. Joseph had now put the young Jesus on top of his shoulders so he could see Sho in the distance. Sho came trotting up to them as if nothing had happened at all and the three of them ran toward the start line, passing the played-out contestants that had dropped in the sand along the way.

Now the crowd was silent. The Romans, the breeders, the Egyptian elites could not believe their eyes. Before them was a mongrel dog that not only won the race but pulled a chariot more than double the distance of the second runner-up. Jesus ran over to Sho and gave him a huge embrace, and that was all Sho wanted in the first place. Now the crowd was restless as they could not even process the fact that a street dog like this could outdo their magnificent Pharaohs.

However, the breeders thought to themselves they would easily win the next leg of the race, for it was designed to measure the speed of a dog. There was no way this big, muscular dog could outrun their beloved Pharaohs. Sho was not in the least worried.

The next day there were only seven dogs in the race. Two had died of heat exhaustion from yesterday's race and the other just wouldn't have any part of the remaining ordeal. But Sho noticed he still had the seventy pound and the giant Pharaoh to contend with. For this race, the chariots were outfitted with a team of two horses. This race would determine the fastest dog in the land. Clearly, Sho was the strongest, but the Pharaoh was designed for speed, not strength, so this should be their event. They had long legs and took huge strides. Their chests were thin and everything about the breed spelled speed.

The chariots would blaze across the Egyptian countryside followed by the dogs. Each chariot had an independent handler of the horses and two people were allowed in the back of the chariot, offering encouragement to their dog. The distance covered was around three miles from beginning to end.

Once again all the chariots were aligned abreast. Joseph and Jesus mounted the chariot with Sho a distance of fifty feet behind them, along with the other six dogs. Again, Sho looked over and saw the giant Pharaoh now fully recovered from yesterday's ordeal. He saw the other big one as well. For this race Sho thought the lighter Pharaoh would be his biggest competition, as they were obviously built for speed. No one gave the overgrown mutt, Sho, a chance to win the speed event.

Joseph wisely tied a rope to the young Jesus and then fastened the other end around his waist. Joseph knew they might reach some very fast speeds from what he had heard about in previous races. Suddenly, just like the day before, the trumpet blew and the teams were off. Joseph could feel the raw power of two horses pulling with all their might to reach a top speed. The feeling was overpowering. At the same time, the dogs were released and were off to catch their owners waving from the backs of the chariots.

Quickly, the lighter ones grabbed a large lead. They cut through the desert air like a falcon swooping in on a kill. They easily had a twenty yard head start on the mighty Sho. The giant and the seventy-pounder were slightly ahead of Sho and they began closing in on the lighter, faster dogs.

Sho at this point was in half stride, but felt this would be the time to make his move. He could hear Jesus shouting his name in the distance and this was all the encouragement he needed to go full stride. This was the secret weapon Sho had that no other dog before or since has had. Other dogs had their legs operating independently. It would look like they were in full stride, but because they moved so fast, you really couldn't tell. Sho, however, would pull from his two front legs while the back legs were reloading, then his back legs would dig in and push forward while his front legs were reloading for another large pull. This had the effect of always having two legs fully in motion, letting the other two rest and reload and on and on it would go. Therefore, Sho was almost twice as fast as any creature on the planet. Only the cheetah could rival him, but just for a short distance. Sho had the stamina to outlast any other creature. God, in his wisdom, had given Sho a heart twice the size of any other dog and this meant double the amount of oxygen going through his arteries to his muscles.

In reality the other dogs never stood a chance. Sho, now in full stride, shot past the seventy pounder, past the other Pharaohs and closed in on the giant in a matter of seconds. Again Sho and the giant were neck and neck with the two chariots some fifty yards away. The horses were now foaming white froth from exhaustion at running at an extreme pace. Sho decided to end the race right there. He put on a final burst, his long legs pulling from the front and pushing from the rear, and within a matter of seconds, reached the same speed of the chariot holding Jesus and Joseph and leaped into the back. Once again Jesus gave Sho the biggest hug he could muster! And that hug from his little friend was all in the world the great Sho wanted.

The other dogs stopped in their tracks as they saw the chariot with Sho disappear into the distance. All those attending the race said that was the only time in race history that a dog ran down a chariot that was pulled by two horses and was able to jump on board.

Sho was now the most popular thing in all the land. Joseph was given the reward of two talents of gold. Then Joseph, Mary, Jesus and Sho headed back to Hepru with the mighty dog returning as a true celebrity.

However, winning this race in the manner in which he did set some very negative things in motion. For one thing, the ruling Roman general in charge of Egypt had now decided he had to have Sho for his personal use. He became obsessed with having Sho. Night and day the devil was working on him to take Sho away from Jesus. He had an emissary go to Hepru with an offer to purchase Sho for the amazing sum of twenty talents of gold! Joseph and Mary didn't even give the offer a minute's thought. News of the family's refusal enraged the general.

Rapidly however, the family's exile in Egypt was coming to an end. Herod had recently died and an angel of the Lord once again appeared in a dream to Joseph and said, *"Get up, take the child and his mother and go to the land of Israel for those who were trying to take the child's life are dead."* Joseph and Mary had become very accepted members of the small Jewish settlement there. All the people went to Joseph when they needed the skills of a carpenter. Mary liked that no one was gossiping about her as they had done in Nazareth. All the women liked Jesus. It was, for Mary, the best time of her life and she found out once again she was pregnant.

The family would be leaving Egypt in several days. Joseph was busy doing repairs on the cart they had brought with them years earlier when they left Israel. Mary was preparing for the trip as well and had to give away many of the things they had accumulated over the years that were just not practical for the long journey ahead of them.

While the family was preparing to rendezvous with a caravan, something terrible happened. The Roman general in charge of Egypt had decided he must have the mighty Sho for his own pleasure so he dispatched a group of Roman soldiers, numbering five, to go to Hepru and take Sho away from his family. As the family was taking a midday break from their tasks of getting things in order, there was a knock at their door. Joseph opened the door and was startled to see Roman soldiers. Without any invitation the commander of the group entered and announced his intention of taking Sho. Immediately Joseph and Mary went into a panic. Sho, sensing something was very wrong, started running around the family's courtyard. Jesus began screaming at the top of his lungs.

The Romans were prepared, however, and four of them cornered Sho and tossed a giant net over him. Now there was nothing Sho could do; he was trapped. They immediately encircled Sho with the net and dragged him outside, where they had a cage mounted on top of a cart. Then as quickly as they had arrived, the Roman detail had vanished. It was impossible to challenge them as they were seasoned soldiers with swords and spears. Joseph was helpless.

That evening was the worst night of the family's history. Mary and Jesus were crying and Joseph was in a state of shock. They would have to leave Egypt without Sho, Joseph thought to himself. The angel's command was to leave Egypt, with or without Sho. Everyone in the family that evening collapsed from exhaustion from all the worry they had felt at the loss of Sho. Jesus especially was heartbroken and it was all Mary could do to console him. Joseph felt the family should leave immediately in the morning in case the Romans returned looking for them.

That morning, as the sun broke over the hills to the east of Hepru, Joseph had the cart all packed and ready. He helped Mary and Jesus onto the cart and they set out for their new life in Israel. Everyone in town lined the street saying their good-byes, and many were weeping knowing the family had lost their wonderful Sho to the Romans.

After several hours of traveling north and east, the family turned around as they reached the last large hill of the fertile Nile valley. In the distance stood the most magnificent sight in the ancient world — the pyramids of Giza. Until yesterday Joseph and Mary loved everything about their stay in Egypt; now they were leaving brokenhearted. As they rounded the last hill where they could no longer see the pyramids, Joseph thought he heard a faint bark. His mind and the desert wind must be playing tricks on him. There could be no dog in this desolate part of Egypt. Again there was another bark. This was surely the unique bark of Sho! Joseph turned around and spotted a black dot coming toward them at breakneck speed, getting larger by the second. Could this be Sho? he thought. He shouted at Mary to turn around. Mary too thought this sounded like Sho. Jesus knew immediately it was Sho and he was jumping up and down in the back of the cart. A couple of minutes later, right before them stood the mighty Sho. He was bloodied and needed water badly, but seemed to have no permanent injury. The grateful family surrounded Sho and smothered him with hugs and kisses! Sho was so happy to be back with his family he collapsed from exhaustion and did not wake up until the next day.

The Roman general was so upset about not getting Sho he sent a hundred men to scour the land to find him. Of course they never did find Joseph, Mary, Jesus and Sho, as they had long left the land of Egypt. And no one knows how, or who, or what, but the Roman soldiers who had captured and kidnapped Sho were never seen alive again after they left the town of Hepru with Sho.

If I speak with the languages of men and of angels, but don't have love, I have become sounding brass, or a clanging cymbal. If I have the gift of prophecy, and know all mysteries and all knowledge; and if I have all faith, so as to remove mountains, but don't have love, I am nothing.

If I dole out all my goods to feed the poor, and if I give my body to be burned, but don't have love, it profits me nothing.

Love is patient and is kind, love doesn't envy. Love doesn't brag, is not proud, doesn't behave itself inappropriately, doesn't seek its own way, is not provoked, takes no account of evil, doesn't rejoice in unrighteousness, but rejoices with the truth, bears all things, believes all things, hopes all things, endures all things.

Love never fails. But where there are prophecies, they will be done away with. Where there are various languages, they will cease. Where there is knowledge, it will be done away with. For we know in part, and we prophesy in part, but when that which is complete has come, then that which is partial will be done away with. When I was a child, I spoke as a child, I felt as a child, I thought as a child. Now that I have become a man, I have put away childish things. For now we see in a mirror, dimly, but then face to face. Now I know in part, but then I will know fully, even as I was also fully known.

But now faith, hope, and love remain—these three. The greatest of these is love. (1 Corinthians 13:1-13)

Chapter 5

Jesus Discovers Love

T he family had now long settled in Nazareth, their old hometown. Joseph had returned to his carpentry business, taking care of the financial aspects of the household. He now had a thriving business, often making business trips to Sepphoris, the Gentile town a couple of hours' walk from Nazareth. Mary was now pregnant with their fourth child and was busy taking care of the ever-busy household. Jesus was occupied learning scripture from the local Hebrew school run by an old rabbi. When Jesus was not in school, or after school, he was helping Joseph with the carpentry business. There was much to learn within both disciplines—one physical, the other spiritual. How fitting that the god/man would be learning trades in the spiritual and physical worlds. One could wonder if it was very difficult for the young Jesus to learn the carpenter trade, knowing his calling would be repairing men—not furniture.

Jesus was now close to his twelfth year and considered a young man. In the ancient world children grew up fast. They had little choice, for life spans were short, averaging forty years for a male. Boys had to learn their father's trade early in their lives, as it was a natural and expected occurrence that a son would take over the family business and care for the entire family, whether it was farming, fishing, teaching, military or carpentry in the case of Jesus.

Sho had passed his prime. The average life span of a dog in the ancient world was a mere four years. But the mighty Sho showed no signs of slowing down. He could still run faster and jump higher than the other dogs. There were only about six dogs in Nazareth and they usually hung out in a single pack. Being a pack member gave them a sense of security and it usually made scraping for the next meal somewhat easier. They weren't as keen as a pack of wolves, but they could inflict serious damage—if needed. The townspeople usually stayed clear of the pack for obvious reasons. Likewise, the pack always stayed clear of Shomer unless he allowed some form of contact to occur. They would change course or run in the opposite direction if they saw or smelled any sign of Sho.

Once when Jesus was eight and headed home from school, the pack began chasing him and acted as if he was to be their next meal. Like a ghost, Sho showed up from nowhere. He bit into the lead dog's tail, snapping it as if it were a tree branch cut in half. The lead dog dropped immediately to its feet when it realized that Sho was the one that had inflicted the damage. The pack knew not to mess with Sho and the rest scattered. Dogs instinctively know when they face a truly powerful canine not to provoke it. (These more powerful dogs came to be known as alpha dogs.) This pack knew Shomer was the alpha male of the village, period! So they quickly dispersed, running off into the field next to where the incident occurred. Jesus was now safe.

Jesus so loved Sho. Sho took the place of a best friend in Jesus's life. It seemed that every one of Jesus's memories involved Sho; the two were inseparable and where you saw one, the other was not far away. This was, as is everything else, planned by God. He knew Jesus would have a difficult life living with humans and would need a friend like Sho; someone he could love and confide in.

Jesus dearly loved the little children of Nazareth. They would come by Joseph's carpentry shop and sing songs with him and listen to stories that Joseph would tell. But in reality the children came to visit Sho. A dog as a pet was very unusual in those times and the children couldn't get over Jesus having an awesome friend like Sho. Of course, Sho ate up all the attention the kids would toss in his direction.

Young Jesus was known to have an amazing memory. Even Joseph was astonished when they were taking measurements for a job and Jesus would measure something once and not even bother to jot down the calculations. Joseph, on the other hand, would measure three times just to make certain he had done it right. Also, Jesus was able to read the Torah (Old Testament) and memorize it. This gift would serve him greatly when he began his ministry. He would have many verbal wars concerning scripture with the Jewish authorities—scribes, priests, Sadducees and Pharisees. As a boy, however, this gift was not appreciated by some of the other boys. They no doubt were jealous of his ability, particularly because he was so modest and never flaunted it. Even the rabbi could not come close to Jesus's insight into the scriptures. Sho would always accompany Jesus to school, which also added to the other boys' jealousy—they didn't have a furry friend like Sho! Dogs were not pets in those days and the idea of Sho being treated like a family member was too foreign to their understanding. For all this, Jesus had a difficult time when he interacted with other children. The misunderstanding was mutual.

After school one day as he was on his way home, Jesus encountered some of the village boys, who began to harass him. They started with name calling. Words such as freak, loner and even bastard were tossed his way. The rumor had been passed down that Jesus's mother was pregnant before she married. There were few in Nazareth who didn't know about it. Such a sin was a great taboo in Jewish culture and some of the local parents were happy to pass this information down to their children as a warning. Jesus was often the recipient of quiet whispers in the background and people would point and laugh at him and spread more rumors.

On one occasion the name calling by village boys got out of hand and they began tossing rocks at Jesus. Several of the rocks hit their mark, knocking Jesus to the ground. Shomer tried to shield Jesus from the rocks and he absorbed the blows from most of them as they landed on his side and head and missed Jesus. As rocks were sailing in from all angles, Sho held his ground and protected his best friend. Finally Sho had enough. He sprang toward the largest boy, perhaps sixteen, pinned him to the ground and had his teeth firmly surrounding the boy's throat. He could have ripped the boy's throat out within seconds, but Jesus yelled, **"Sho, stop!"** Sho eased his grip; his master had issued a one word command, "Stop!" He froze instantly, waiting for the next command. Jesus walked up to Sho and pulled him off the boy. The other boys, shaking in fear, dropped their rocks. Jesus looked up and said to the boys, **"And why do you persecute me?"** The oldest boy, who had started the trouble and who Sho had attacked, began to weep. Jesus knew the older boy was not from Nazareth and asked his name. "My name is Barabbas and I'm here to visit family," he answered. Whether it was the recognition that his life had just been spared or the power of the question that Jesus had just posed, the boy got up and ran down the street, never to confront Jesus again. Little did either of them know at the time that their paths would cross again some twenty years in the future. Jesus, at the age of twelve, was beginning to get a glimpse of his mission in life. How ironic that years later Jesus would pose the same question to someone more powerful than a group of village boys.

Jesus and Sho returned home after the incident, both bloodied and bruised. Mary was furious and quite ready to confront the parents of the boys. Joseph, however, seemed to understand the valuable nature of the lesson learned by the young Jesus. He knew this incident would serve him well as a man, knowing that some people are just plain mean and vindictive. Joseph then decided it was best to let the event pass without creating problems within the little hamlet.

The greatest crisis of Jesus's youth occurred on a late summer day a year after the attack by the village boys. The day was like most summer days in Nazareth, with their warm afternoons and cool evenings accompanied by a slight breeze. That morning Joseph and Jesus decided to go visit their family food plot. They had around five acres of land that had been handed down from generation to generation, where they planted vegetables, grapes for wine, olives, dates and Jesus's favorite—figs. Jesus was a vegetarian by nature. He abhorred eating animal flesh, although he did not pass judgment on those who did. He loved fruits and vegetables and fish. Over the years, he and Sho would often make trips to the Sea of Galilee to spend time together fishing.

That morning Joseph, Jesus and Sho left the house with high expectations of collecting figs and other foods to bring home. Joseph and Jesus each had a basket to fill, although Jesus's basket was smaller. When they reached the acreage, they went their separate ways. Sho decided to chase rabbits along the hillside that overlooked the land. Sho loved to hunt and most of his life he fed himself by hunting, but he was always careful to keep Jesus within eyesight. Joseph went another direction to pick olives and Jesus went straight ahead, making a beeline for some fig trees growing at the back of the plot. He wasted little time filling his basket; it made him feel good to know he was helping the family gather food. He knew his mother would be happy to see his basket overflowing with ripe figs. Now that Mary was pregnant again, Jesus tried to help his mother in every way possible.

Jesus bent over to collect the last of his figs and he could see from the corner of his eye something moving. Suddenly he found himself within six feet and face to face with an eight-foot-long king cobra. It was black as night and had piercing red eyes. Jesus had heard that this venomous snake was found in more desertlike areas, but he had never seen one. The snake uncoiled and rose into the air, ready to strike. It hissed as it rose higher. The snake was possessed by Satan and its mission was to take the life of Jesus. Satan was given dominion over the Earth and he intended to emerge triumphant today and stop God's plan for the young boy. Jesus did not move—he had been warned about such creatures. Out of fear and instinct Jesus yelled as loud as his voice and lungs would permit, **"Sho, help!"**

Sho was about fifty yards away and stopped hunting immediately, zeroed his eyes toward Jesus and saw the snake weaving its head side to side, aimed directly at Jesus. Sho immediately ran faster than he ever had in his life. Jesus couldn't take his eyes off the snake to look for Sho; he could only hope Sho had heard his plea. Joseph heard Jesus's cry, but was too far away to help. Suddenly from a distance of about four feet the snake struck, aiming for Jesus's throat. But Sho, seeing death so close, dug in his massive hind legs and leapt from a distance of twenty feet and intercepted the blow. He had covered the entire distance in less than two seconds. The cobra and Sho met in midair, both weightless for a few seconds, then Sho snapped off the snake's head.

However, the snake had found a mark—not Jesus, but Sho. The snake had clamped down on Sho's tongue thinking it was Jesus's throat. It pumped all its deadly venom directly into Sho's bloodstream. Even in death the body of the snake was able to wrap itself around Sho, trying to squeeze the life from him. It didn't have to wait long. Within two minutes the mighty Shomer's breathing stopped and he gazed into Jesus's eyes as if to say good-bye. Jesus dropped to his knees as he realized his beloved Sho was dead. Jesus had never known death. He had witnessed death a few times in the village, but it had never felt like this. He felt a dear gift had been taken away and he instinctively raised himself up and uncoiled the headless cobra from the body of Sho. He unclamped the head of the viper from Sho's tongue and tossed it to the side. Even in death the snake's head was hissing and its red eyes still ablaze. As he wept uncontrollably over the lifeless body of Sho, his tears drenched the face and eyes of his best friend.

Joseph reached the scene as quickly as possible, but found he was too late to be of help. He saw the cobra's headless body and pieced together what had happened. He, too began to weep as he saw the suffering of Jesus. He also loved Shomer and the burden for both was overpowering. Minutes passed, but they seemed like hours. Joseph had never seen Jesus cry before like this and it was painful to see such innocence grow up so fast. How cruel life could be, Joseph thought. How could Jesus continue without his precious Sho? As Joseph put his arms around Jesus to console him, he noticed something very strange. Was that Sho's tail moving? No, it must be the breeze that caught the hairs at the end of the dog's tail, he thought. He wiped the tears from his eyes and focused again on the tail. "No," Joseph knew this was not the wind! He could see Sho's tail was slowly moving; Joseph couldn't believe what he was seeing. Sho took in a deep breath, opened his eyes and let out a little cry and began licking the face of Jesus. The amazing dog's body, with its extra powerful immune system and God's help, had been stronger than the cobra's poison! Now the tears in Jesus's and Joseph's eyes were tears of joy. They looked at each other and only one thing came to mind: *Greater love has no man than this, than he lay down his life for his friend!* Sho wasn't a man, but he had been willing to do what the scripture had extolled—to lay down one's life for another. What a lesson was learned that day; what a message they would take back to Mary. And the world would later see how this sacrificial love would pour itself out for mankind through this young man named Jesus.

God, therefore, in his infinite wisdom had chosen a four-legged creature, born of a homeless stray, to show his Son the true meaning of love. God understood that there was no purer expression of love on earth than that of a boy and his dog. And God, in his infinite wisdom, did not wish it revealed to Jesus that he was God's son until he had first discovered the true meaning of love!

So it was on that summer day, on the family food plot that Jesus discovered the meaning of love and the world and Jesus would never be the same.

Joseph wondered the remainder of his life, was it God that brought Sho back to life or the tears of Jesus?

Then Jesus came from Galilee to the Jordan to John, to be baptized by him. But John would have hindered him saying, "I need to be baptized by you, and you come to me?"

*But Jesus, answering, said to him, **"Allow it now, for this is the fitting way for us to fulfill all righteousness."** Then he allowed him. Jesus, when he was baptized, went up directly from the water: and behold, the heavens were opened to him. He saw the Spirit of God descending as a dove, and coming on him. Behold, a voice out of the heavens said, "This is my beloved Son, with whom I am well pleased." (Matthew 3:13-17)*

Chapter 6

The Ministry Begins

Jesus was now in his prime at the age of thirty. He and Sho had spent the last fifteen years traveling within what is now Asia Minor and India. At the age of fifteen Jesus had felt an overwhelming urge to leave Nazareth and explore the world. There was nothing left for Jesus in Nazareth. More importantly, he had learned everything there was to know about the Jewish faith. No teacher or rabbi in the land had his knowledge and complete understanding of the Hebrew text as did Jesus. It was natural for him to want to expand the center of his own universe, so the next fifteen years would take him and Sho to Asia Minor, Babylon, India and Egypt to study their religious ways and philosophies.

Upon returning to Nazareth, many things had changed. Joseph was now dead. Jesus was very saddened to learn this, as he had a great love for Joseph.

Joseph had instilled in him all the qualities of being a man and although Jesus never had any ambitions of taking over the family's business, over the years he was known to repair quite a few things in his travels. Many times he paid for room and board by trading his skills as a craftsman for a dry place to sleep and a warm meal. Jesus felt work was good for the soul and many of his meditations were done while fixing a chair or building a table. **"The hands have the ability to liberate the mind,"** he would often say.

The family and their friends had a big homecoming party for Jesus when he returned. They sang and danced until the late hours. Mary was so proud to see her firstborn in his prime. Now at the age of thirty he stood a little over six feet tall, easily towering above everyone else, as the average height in his day was around 5'6" for a man. He had shoulder length brown hair and sported a dark, short beard. Jesus's most notable feature was his piercing blue eyes. It was very rare in that part of the world to have blue eyes. His eyes seemed to be able to cut right into your heart and see instantly what you were really about. Many of his enemies soon learned of this power and they quickly learned not to confront Jesus face to face; more often than not they would look down to the ground when addressing Jesus.

Sho on the other hand was now an old, old dog. No dog in human history had ever lived to the age of thirty. He could barely see, for he had cataracts covering his eyes. Somehow enough light seeped through the opaque coverings that he could make his way around, but the going was difficult. His sense of hearing was almost gone. He walked with a noticeable limp and for the last two years while Jesus and Sho were traveling, Jesus created a portable lean-to from buffalo leather stretched between two long poles, which Sho could lie on. Jesus would either pull it himself or use a donkey. Sho was still jet-black, although he did have a fair amount of gray around his muzzle. He had very few teeth left. His tongue would often droop outside his mouth, a side effect of the cobra encounter years earlier. The only sense he hadn't lost over the years was his sense of smell. This sense was still serving him well and he could pretty much tell what was going on around him just by lifting his nose toward the wind. He was often seen standing on all fours with his nose high in the air to take a reading of things.

After the visit with family and old friends, Jesus informed his mother he would be leaving again to begin what he said was **"my time to reach out to the world."** Mary really didn't know what this meant, but patiently decided that it would be revealed to her when the time was right.

With their good-byes behind them, Jesus and Sho set off for a meeting with John the Baptist. The Baptist was easily the most talked about person in all of Israel. Jesus and John were cousins and well acquainted with one another at one time, although it had been many years since they had seen one another. They were born within months of each other and as children their families would get together once a year. This was always a fun time for Jesus, as he didn't have friends his age in Nazareth. John liked Sho a lot and was always a little jealous that Jesus had such a magnificent friend. Their favorite game was to play hide and seek. Jesus and John would run off to a distant field, or a small cave. Sho had to find the boys within an agreed upon time limit. Friendly bets were placed, usually something simple like a household item, and Joseph would command Sho to go and find the boys. Joseph always won the contests, but Sho and the boys loved this adventure. On one occasion they climbed to the top of an old olive tree thinking Sho could never find them so high up in a tree. But only minutes after they made it to the top here comes Sho, nose in the air and homing in on his quarry. The two boys thought they finally got the best of Sho as there was no way he would know they were in a tree. Minutes later Sho was at the base of the tree and let out a loud bark to let them know they had been discovered. This was one of the memories Jesus was carrying with him on his journey to meet John.

Jesus and Sho now set out for the Jordan River. The Jordan gave life to that region of the world. Rolling out from the mountains to the north, it wound its way through the Galilean countryside, where it eventually dumped into the Sea of Galilee. There would be no lake without the Jordan River. This is where John was doing his baptisms.

Jesus didn't know exactly where John would be, but figured that the crowds of people would be a good indicator that John would be near.

Sho was really beginning to worry that his usefulness to Jesus had passed. Jesus, of course, never felt this way, but the prideful Sho was certain he could no longer protect Jesus as he did when he was younger. If he must he would try and rise to the occasion, but secretly he hoped he would not be put in that position. It was a sad sight to see Jesus pulling the lean-to with Sho riding on top across the Galilean countryside. Sho's exploits were well-known in the ancient world and to see him crumpled up like this was heartbreaking. But anyone that has had a dog reach old age knows the look and the heartbreak.

The distance from Nazareth to the section of Jordan River where John might be was about fifty miles. This would easily be a two-day trip for Jesus, but having to pull Sho extended the trip by five more days. Jesus was in incredible shape and was known to all as an avid hiker. He could easily walk twenty miles a day if need be. He loved to walk. Sho and Jesus had walked thousands of miles in their thirty years together. That now had changed.

Jesus began noticing that crowds of people were becoming heavier and heavier as he got near a section of the Jordan called Bethabara. This was the current location where John was baptizing people. It was situated in the lower Jordan Valley. Finally Jesus and Sho turned a final bend on the river and there was John the Baptist with scores of people waiting to be baptized. Jesus set up camp away from the crowds, intending to see the Baptist the next day.

Jesus was very tired from the trip, as he had pulled his friend all the way from Nazareth to the Jordan. That night Jesus split his meager dinner with Sho. Sho didn't eat much these days, but always considered it a special treat when Jesus hand fed him, which he did this evening. Sho couldn't chase game anymore and was fully reliant on Jesus to feed him daily. Sho was a very proud dog and didn't like Jesus's having to do this for him. That night Sho and Jesus lay down together as they had done on hundreds of other occasions. Jesus put his arms around his old crippled friend and said a prayer for Sho. They fell asleep together under the watchful eyes of the stars above the Jordan.

Midmorning the next day Jesus made his way to John, who was already busy in the process of baptizing people. Immediately John saw Jesus coming toward him and said, *"Behold, the Lamb of God, who takes away the sin of the world! This is he of whom I said, 'After me comes a man who is preferred before me, for he was before me.' I didn't know him, but for this reason I came baptizing in water: that he would be revealed to Israel."*

Then John recognized Jesus. He could not tell that the dog with Jesus was Sho. They had not seen each other for over fifteen years. John took Jesus's hand and led him to deeper water. Then in an instant John immersed Jesus under the water of the Jordan for several seconds. Jesus went under the water as a man, but surfaced as God.

Sho became overly excited at all the activity and jumped into the river and swam toward Jesus. Jesus was barely under the water and it sent alarm bells off in Sho's head. Jesus must be in trouble. Just as quickly as Jesus had disappeared under the water, he reappeared with his arms outstretched toward Heaven, then a spirit descended on his head in the shape of a dove. In reality it was a collection of light photons that resembled a dove. Then a voice came out from the heavens saying, *"This is my beloved Son, with whom I am well pleased."* John gave Jesus a big hug and they made their way to the bank. Sho quickly followed. Sho could not seem to restrain himself and tried in vain to capture the bird of light. A couple of times he took perfect aim on the dove as it hovered around Jesus. Sho kept swatting at the mysterious light-form. Every time he was able to zero in on it, his paw would simply pass through the dove, and Sho did not know what to make of this. Even though this was such a sacred moment, both Jesus and John laughed as hard as ever as Sho was trying to catch the Spirit of God.

God was showing Jesus that even in a sacred moment as this it was all right to be human and laugh. Once again God used a simple, four-legged creature to teach a lesson.

Sho, however, was not done with the light bird. He persisted in trying to catch it, running in circles around Jesus and barking wildly. Jesus was happy to see the spark again in his old friend. Jesus was at the moment the happiest he had been in his entire life. His heavenly father was "well pleased" with him and his best friend Sho was showing life again. It was a convergence of love, just for love's sake. No points to be made—just pure love. Jesus would never feel this again in his entire life at this level, and for a brief moment, time seemed to stop and Jesus soaked it all in.

As the light bird left Jesus, Sho decided to give chase. The spirit made a quick retreat downriver and Sho followed. The spectrum of light emitted by the spirit seemed to penetrate Sho's cataracts so he was able to see where he was going. The adrenalin over-rode his arthritis and he disappeared around the river bend, heading up over a ridge into the desert. Jesus could hear him barking, but the sound became more and more faint and finally it completely disappeared. Jesus had little doubt he'd return soon; he always had before. But minutes turned to hours and then nightfall set in. Jesus spent that evening with John and his disciples talking about Herod and Rome and religion, but you could see Jesus was not engaged in any of the conversations as he was too worried about his beloved Sho.

This was the first night in Jesus's life that Sho would not be sleeping by his side. Jesus looked into the face of God in the form of the night sky and offered a prayer to keep Sho safe. He prayed so hard he passed out from exhaustion. Jesus had many odd dreams that evening, but the most comforting was a dream that his work to follow would be hard and difficult, but he could always see Sho by his side.

The next morning as the sun was rising upon the banks of the Jordan River, Jesus was awakened by a familiar lick on his face. Sho had returned! Jesus jumped for joy and gave his friend a hug for the ages! Sho was so excited to reunite with Jesus, his tail was moving back and forth so fast it made a swishing sound as it cut through the air.

But Sho had radically changed. Now he was pure white, like a blistering white summer cloud. He again had all his teeth. His cataracts had disappeared and you could see your reflection in his eyes. Now he could hear the snap of a twig from a hundred yards away. Now he could jump even farther than the time when he was young and jumped from the bank of the Nile onto the back of the croc about to devour Jesus. God had performed a miracle on Sho and Jesus stared in disbelief as his best friend was in his prime again. **"All things are possible by the Father,"** he said. It took some getting used to seeing Sho in a fur of pure white, but somehow being in the presence of God all night had turned his coat white. In an act of joy Jesus ripped apart the lean-to, tossing it on the fire, and began dancing around the camp as it turned into ashes! John's disciples thought he had gone crazy, but he and Sho knew better.

Jesus, full of the Holy Spirit, returned from the Jordan, and was led by the Spirit into the wilderness for forty days, being tempted by the devil. He ate nothing in those days. Afterward, when they were completed, he was hungry. The devil said to him, "If you are the Son of God, command this stone to become bread."

Jesus answered him, saying, **"It is written, 'Man shall not live by bread alone, but by every word of God.'"** *(Luke 4:1-4)*

Chapter 7

Temptation and Rejection

Sho was loving life again now that he had his new body, although he did take note he was now white and not black. He didn't understand why or how this was, just that once again he had the speed to outrun a lion, had the legs to jump alongside the gazelles and with his new eyes could again see the flicker of a rabbit's ear a hundred yards away! God's spirit had renewed him to his youth and for this Jesus was so thankful. For the first time in their lives Jesus and Sho were in their prime together. There had always been a large age gap between the two of them, but it never affected their love for one another. Jesus was now a man in his prime and Sho was a magnificent creature in his prime. Together they were ready to make history.

Sho wondered what was taking them to the desert above the Dead Sea. Jesus had found a cave that had a small but steady flow of water coming out of the rocks. He informed Sho this would be their home for the next forty days. Sho was puzzled why they would ever want to stay here overnight, much less forty days, be he knew Jesus had his reasons, so he resolved to make the best of it all. Jesus immediately began meditating. Over the years Sho had seen Jesus in this state many times, especially after their years in India, but never to this extent. He had seen his Master fast many times as well, but never this length of time. It was the most boring forty days of his life. His best friend seemed disconnected from his very existence. Jesus wasn't singing, or dancing, or playing their favorite game of fetch. Sho loved to fetch any object Jesus would toss. But now, during this time, there was none of that. He thought he'd be patient and see how long Jesus would be occupied with this boring routine at this ugly spot in the desert. The best Sho could do was go hunting in the early morning before it got too hot. There wasn't much to hunt or chase in this desolate portion of the desert, but fortunately each morning there was plenty of this white stuff to eat. Jesus called it manna and it provided Sho all the nourishment he would need.

Then one day, after weeks of prayer and meditation a black cobra the size and shape of the one that attacked Jesus when he was a boy appeared before Jesus. The snake stopped several feet short of Jesus and immediately Sho jumped in front of Jesus to protect him. This brought memories of the snake attack on Jesus years earlier and Sho felt this time he knew what to do. Jesus, however, laid his shepherd's staff in front of the snake and it halted its advance. The staff of Jesus began to transform into a snake also. As the two snakes were sizing each other up, the black cobra with the blazing red eyes transformed itself and began to take on something of a human form.

Jesus and Satan were now face-to-face. Jesus bent down and touched the tail of the snake and it immediately transformed back into his staff.

"I see you have the staff of Moses and Aaron," Satan uttered. "I also see you still have the dog I killed in the field years ago," he uttered again.

"Yes you did kill him and he you, but the power of God brought life into him and behold he lives," Jesus said to Satan.

"The devil, leading him up on a high mountain, showed him all the kingdoms of the world in a moment of time. The devil said to him, 'I will give you all this authority, and their glory, for it has been delivered to me; and I give it to whomever I want. If you therefore will worship before me, it will all be

yours.' Jesus answered him, **'Get behind me Satan!**
For it is written, 'You shall worship the Lord your
God, and him only shall you serve.'

"He led him to Jerusalem, and set him on the
pinnacle of the temple, and said to him, 'If you are
the Son of God, cast yourself down from here, for
it is written, "He will give his angels charge concerning you, to guard you;" and, "On their hands
they will bear you up, lest perhaps you dash your
foot against a stone."

Jesus, answering, said to him, **"It has been said,**
'You shall not tempt the Lord your God.'"

When the devil had completed every temptation,
he departed from him until another time.

Sho was visibly upset that Jesus would just disappear that way. Although he was only gone a few
minutes, for Sho it seemed a lifetime being away
from his Master.

Not soon after the encounter with Satan, Jesus
returned, gave Sho a huge hug, roughed up his ears
a little and gave the command Sho had been longing
for: **"Sho let's get up and go back to Nazareth."**
Sho couldn't wait to leave this place and took the
lead as he always had as they began the trek from the
desert surrounding the Dead Sea.

Jesus returned in the power of the Spirit into Galilee and news about him spread through all the surrounding area. He taught in their synagogues, being glorified by all.

He came to Nazareth, where he had been brought up. He entered, as was his custom, into the synagogue on the Sabbath day and stood up to read. The book of the prophet Isaiah was handed to him. He opened the book and found the place where it was written:

"The Spirit of the Lord is on me, because he has anointed me to preach good news to the poor. He has sent me to heal the brokenhearted, to proclaim release to the captives, recovering of sight to the blind, to deliver those who are crushed, and to proclaim the acceptable year of the Lord."

He closed the book, gave it back to the attendant and sat down. Everyone in the synagogue had their eyes riveted on Jesus. He began to tell them, *"Today this Scripture has been fulfilled in your hearing."*

People present talked openly about Jesus and were mesmerized by his words of wisdom and someone shouted out from the crownd, "Isn't this Joseph's son?"

He said to them, *"Doubtless you will tell me this parable, 'Physician, heal yourself! Whatever we have heard done at Capernaum, do also here in your hometown.'" He said, "Most certainly I tell you, no prophet is acceptable in his hometown. But truly I tell you, there were many widows in Israel in the days of Elijah, when the sky was shut up three years and six months, when a great famine came over all the land. Elijah was sent to none of them, except to Zarephath, in the land of Sidon, to a woman who was a widow. There were many lepers in Israel in the time of Elisha the prophet, yet not one of them was cleansed, except Naaman, the Syrian."*

They were all filled with wrath in the synagogue, as they heard these things. They rose up, threw him out of the city and led him to the brow of the hill that their city was built on, that they might throw him off the cliff...

Up until now Sho was sitting in the back of the synagogue listening to his Master talk. Sho had learned to be a good listener of humans and especially Jesus. He learned years ago, however, that humans talk differently when they become excited. The pitch in the voice would rise; this is when Sho would take note of the voice of a stranger. He had learned over the years that an excited human voice would more often than not lead to danger. He also had learned that when humans get excited, they emit an odor that was like nothing else known in the natural world.

He was beginning to get a whiff of that odor as the crowd began yelling.

Before he knew it, the entire crowd had surrounded Jesus and was moving as one unit toward the cliff on the outskirts of town. This was a steep drop-off into a wadi of over one hundred feet. For decades the town used this as their garbage dump. Sho had become separated from Jesus because of the large number of people and he had the distinct feeling his Master was now in trouble! The leaders of the crowd approached the edge of the cliff and were preparing to toss Jesus over. Sho muscled his way through the mob, made a huge leap knocking down two people and landed right in front of Jesus.

Now it was clear to everyone that to get to Jesus they would have to go through this white dog. Sho's powers and exploits were very well-known to everyone in the village. Everyone present knew the story of how some years earlier Sho had killed two male rogue lions that had passed through Nazareth. They knew the story of the crocs from the Nile, as did most of the world. They knew the story of the king cobra in the family field years ago, but no one knew God brought Sho back to life except Joseph and Mary and of course, Jesus.

In a split moment, with Sho flashing his brand new razor-sharp teeth, his back arched, ready to rip open the throat of the next person who touched his Master, the leaders of the mob backed down... *"and he, passing through the midst of them, went his way."* Jesus walked straight ahead and did not look back; Sho, right behind Jesus, gave an occasional glance back at the mob and uttered a firm growl not to follow them. Sho had saved the life of Jesus one more time. With a sense of purpose they marched forward to fulfill their destinies and left Jesus's hometown of Nazareth, never looking back.

The third day, there was a marriage in Cana of Galilee. Jesus's mother was there. Jesus also was invited, with his disciples, to the marriage. When the wine ran out, Jesus's mother said to him, "They have no wine."

Jesus said to her, **"Woman, what does that have to do with you and me? My hour has not yet come."**

His mother said to the servants, "Whatever he says to you, do it." (John 2:1-5)

Chapter 8

Keep the Wine Flowing

Cana was another tiny village in Galilee, and a village Jesus was fond of. It was located approximately five miles south of the bustling Sepphoris. Sepphoris was a large town and much trade and commerce was located there. Cana was more or less a bedroom community and housed a couple hundred families.

Few things were taken as seriously in life as a Jewish wedding and this one was extra special for Jesus, as one of his family members was the bride. Of course the entire family must be there and that included Jesus. Mary was adamant that Jesus attend so she had one of her sons comb the countryside looking for him. By now Jesus wasn't that difficult to find as word of his "last stop" always spread like wildfire throughout the land.

A wedding and the associated feast might go on for a week. For a family to fail in being hospitable during this time was very taboo. Certainly running out of wine during the period of the wedding feast would be a major disaster and considered an insult to friends and family!

This was the first Mary had seen of Sho is his new white coat. She didn't know what to make of it and asked Jesus how this came about. Jesus passed on the story of Sho's encounter with God's Spirit and she simply smiled in understanding. She had loved Sho from a puppy and Sho loved Mary equally. Sho walked up to Mary and gave her a big lick, his way of showing affection. Mary bent down and gave Sho a huge hug. The movement of Sho's tail was acknowledgement of how he felt about Mary.

Because of the unexpected number of people that showed for the wedding, the host family, of which Mary was part of, ran out of wine. This was a huge embarrassment for the family and something had to be done immediately. Then Mary, knowing some of the powers of Jesus, cornered him and insisted he do something to alleviate the problem. Jesus did not want to waste his powers on something like this, but because his mother was so upset at the proposition of being out of wine for all guests, he gave in.

At the wedding festival venue there were six water pots of stone set aside so people could wash their hands; this method of purifying was very important to the Jews.

So, with the family's pride and reputation on the line, Jesus said to them, *"Fill the water pots with water."* They filled them up to the brim. He said to them, *"Now draw some out and take it to the ruler of the feast."*

So they took it. When the ruler of the feast tasted the water now became wine and didn't know where it came from (but the servants who had drawn the water knew), the ruler of the feast called the bridegroom and said to him, "Everyone serves the good wine first, and when the guests have drunk freely, then that which is worse. You have kept the good wine until now!"

Seated at one end of a long table was the bride and groom and at the other end Jesus was seated, as he was the guest of honor. Jesus insisted that a chair be provided to Sho so he could also sit at the wedding table. This rubbed many of the guests the wrong way as no one had ever had a dog seated at a dinner table, much less at a wedding feast. But Jesus was always trying to prove a point to people to think outside of their normal world and this would be another golden opportunity for him to do so.

Sho was loving every moment of the party. People were singing and dancing and making speeches, but most of all there was lots of food. There was the usual assortment of fruits and vegetables, but for this occasion lots of meats: fish, beef, lamb and Sho's favorite, rabbit.

Toward the end of the evening, each guest at the table would make a toast to the bride and groom, followed by a healthy swallow of wine, and everyone would cheer!

Then it came time for Jesus to make a toast and he said the following as he put his arms around Sho, giving him a giant embrace. Jesus stood up, raised his cup of wine and said, **"It is my hope that every man know the conditional love of a woman, and the unconditional love of a dog."**

Suddenly there was dead silence around the room as no one could figure out what Jesus meant. Several seconds later, those attending burst out into applause, mostly as a gesture to be polite to Jesus.

Later that evening Mary approached her son and asked what he meant by the statement. Jesus simply put his arms around his mother and thanked her for being there for him all these years. It was here in Cana that Jesus had performed his first miracle.

It was later said by those at the feast this was the finest wine they had ever tasted and must have come from Heaven. Little did they know!

After this (his miracle in Cana), he went down to Capernaum, he, and his mother, his brothers, and his disciples; and they stayed there a few days. The Passover of the Jews was at hand, and Jesus went up to Jerusalem.

*He found in the temple those who sold oxen, sheep, and doves, and the changers of money sitting. He made a whip of cords, and threw all out of the temple, both the sheep and the oxen; and he poured out the changers' money, and overthrew their tables. To those who sold the doves, he said, **"Take these things out of here! Don't make my Father's house a marketplace!"** (John 2:12-16)*

Chapter 9

Clearing the Temple

J esus felt it was now time to confront the religious authorities and lay down the gauntlet. He also knew they were not going to bow down quietly. With all the authority of God on his side, Jesus headed straight for the inner court of the Temple area in Jerusalem. Of course, Sho was next to Jesus on his right side. Positioned directly at the center of this area was a large altar, a laver, the slaughterhouse and numerous tables where the offerings were prepared.

Like a beam of light, Jesus headed straight for the money changers or those selling animals for sacrifice. Jesus spotted some ropes from the corner of his eye and quickly grabbed a couple. Using his handyman skills, he frayed the ropes at their ends and tied the ropes to the end of his shepherd's staff. This made a very effective whip. Quickly he snapped the whip and the crack of the whip echoed throughout the Temple, gaining the attention of everyone.

To the right of Jesus was a Temple security detail of two men. Weapons were not allowed in the temple area, but they did have two huge dogs. These dogs were veterans of the Coliseum in Rome and had seen much death and inflicted their share themselves. They were given to Pontius Pilate by the Emperor Tiberius. As a good gesture Pilate gave them to the Sanhedrin to be used for Temple security. The handlers of these two fierce beasts were retired gladiators and the dogs were trained to respond to their every command. Sho quickly sized them up. They both had numerous scars along the sides of their bodies. One was missing an eye. Both sported huge chain collars around their necks with a six-foot chain lead. Sho had never seen this breed of dog before, but guessed their weight to be around one hundred fifty pounds each. They were the biggest dogs he had ever seen.

The dogs let out a couple of loud barks when they saw Jesus go after the men who were selling animals for sacrifice. This was new, Sho thought to himself, as he had never seen Jesus get angry like this before. Therefore he had to do a balancing act: one eye trained on Jesus to see how this was going to end up and the other on the two "death dogs." Sho ran alongside Jesus as he upended tables, tossed chairs across the courtyard, smashed cages and upended jars of coins the money changers were filling. People were scattering everywhere.

The handlers of the "death dogs" were in a panic as to what to do and then Caiaphas shot over from across the temple and pointed at the men to do something about Jesus. They were about to unleash the dogs when Sho ran across the courtyard directly in front of them. Sho gave them a low growl that sounded like it came from the depths of Hell itself. Then he curled his upper lips exposing his most amazing teeth (truly lethal weapons), raised his right leg as high as he had ever done before and urinated a steady stream two feet in front of the pair, seemingly daring them to make a move. When he finished he stared at them, tail straight, back arched, ready for a showdown. The handlers, of course, knew of the reputation of Sho. They had never seen Sho before, but they, like everyone else in the ancient world, had heard stories about the dog of Jesus. They didn't want to be responsible for the deaths of these two dogs that the Emperor had given Pilate. So in unison the dog's handlers and the "death dogs" backed down, for now. The dogs lowered their heads in a sign of submission and the handlers pulled tight on their chain lead.

Sho backed down the steps so as not to turn his back on the pair. He knew they had backed down for the moment, but still did not trust animals of that kind.

After all the chaos had settled down, the Temple Jews demanded of him, *"What sign do you show us, seeing that you do these things?"*

Jesus answered them, **"Destroy this temple and in three days I will raise it up."**

The Jews replied, *"Forty-six years was this temple in building, and will you raise it up in three days?" But he spoke of the temple of his body. When therefore he was raised from the dead, his disciples remembered that he said this, and they believed the Scripture, and the word which Jesus had said.*

Now when he was in Jerusalem at the Passover, during the feast, many believed in his name, observing his signs which he did.

All the while Caiaphas and others of the Sanhedrin were watching and listening to Jesus speak. It was right then and there they knew Jesus was going to be a real threat to their world order and something must be done to be rid of Jesus of Nazareth.

It happened in these days, that he went out to the mountain to pray, and he continued all night in prayer to God. When it was day, he called his disciples, and from them he chose twelve, whom he also named apostles: Simon, whom he also named Peter; Andrew his brother; James; John; Philip; Bartholomew; Matthew; Thomas; James, the son of Alphaeus; Simon, who was called the Zealot; Judas the son of James; and Judas Iscariot, who also became a traitor. (Luke 6:12-16)

Chapter 10

The Twelve

Now Jesus and Sho made haste from Jerusalem toward Capernaum. As the sun was setting in the west, Jesus found a nice spot to spend the night amid a grove of olive trees. Usually being near an olive grove meant there would be people about, but Sho sniffed the air and couldn't catch a scent of anyone. Neither Jesus nor Sho knew this would be their last night spent alone.

It had been a difficult day for the both of them. Jesus reflected on the people of Nazareth who had turned on him. This incident gave Jesus a real glimpse of the difficulty that would await him in trying to save mankind from itself. The incidents in Jerusalem and Nazareth were a painful lesson about how religious fervor could turn otherwise civilized people into fanatics.

Sho began to notice a change in Jesus. Sometimes he would begin talking to someone, but there was no one visibly around. He was quite certain of this as he couldn't see or smell anyone, but Jesus would have complete conversations with someone or something. This puzzled Sho, but Jesus seemed quite relaxed and at peace when he was having these conversations, so he let it pass and didn't give it much thought.

That night under the starlit Galilean sky, Jesus and Sho lay down to sleep. As was usually the case Sho rolled up close on the side of Jesus to help keep him warm. As was his custom, after a couple of hours Sho would wake up, stretch, then walk around to the other side of Jesus and lie down to make sure Jesus stayed warm on his other side. But this would be the last night of their lives they would be alone. For thirty years now Sho had always had Jesus pretty much to himself. Now that was changing fast as Jesus had more and more crowds following him. Jesus was now very much a public figure. Everyone seemed to want a piece of Jesus for one thing or another and sought him out.

It was now apparent to Jesus he would need help to manage his ministry. Everywhere he went crowds tried to envelop him. They wanted him to heal their sick, feed their poor, expel demons and perform other miracles. Therefore Jesus prayed about what to do and decided that just like the twelve tribes of ancient Israel he would have twelve disciples to help him spread the word, sharing in the workload.

So *Jesus went up into the mountain, and called to himself those whom he wanted, and they went to him. He appointed twelve, that they might be with him, and that he might send them out to preach, and to have authority to heal sicknesses and to cast out demons.*

Now Sho not only had to deal with these large crowds, but he had to break in these twelve Jesus had decided to be his inner circle. Many of them were fishermen, which Sho liked. Many times in their youth, Jesus and Sho would trek to the Sea of Galilee on fishing trips. Sho always loved to fish with Jesus and they had many wonderful days together at the lake.

As each new disciple showed up to their camp, Sho would engage in a ritual of first barking at them (just to see if they were comfortable with dogs), then walking up to them and smelling them. Everyone had to pass the smell test. Jesus would just sit back and watch with wonder at the test Sho would impose on each of his new disciples. Each of the disciples passed the smell test except one and he was the one called Judas Iscariot. Something was not right with this one. He had the smell of a man who was conflicted and therefore not to be trusted. Sho decided this was a human he would keep a very close eye on. It is one of the awesome traits dogs have of being able to judge a person's character—truly a sixth sense.

On the flip side of things, Sho loved having new people around to play with. Jesus was not spending that much time with him these days—too many people wanting too many things of Jesus. So Sho started to find new friends among the twelve. He decided early on his favorite of the twelve was Peter as he was a person who seemed to always live in the moment. He was loud, had a boisterous laugh and in general just seemed to enjoy life. Peter also took to Sho. One day Jesus noticed Peter and Sho were playing fetch with a papyrus ball. Jesus knew Sho could do this all day and never slow down. But he thought he would put Peter to the test and see who would give in first. The outcome was never in doubt as a couple of hours later Peter threw his hands into the air, giving up and let Sho know he had won the day. Jesus just smiled.

Jesus decided each of the disciples would have certain responsibilities. He then divided the group to handle three major tasks that needed attending each day.

First, they always needed a place to sleep for the evening. So he charged Andrew, Philip and Bartholomew with the task of finding either a good campsite for the group or rooms when they were in a town. The group camped out many times, and a good campsite must include a fresh water source, plenty of firewood and protection from the elements if possible.

Second, he charged Matthew, Thomas, James, Thaddaeus and Simon the Zealot with procuring food for everyone. This was not easy when they were out in the field but much easier when they were staying in a town. Additionally, they had to find food for the many people who followed Jesus around.

Thirdly, Peter, James and John were head of security for the group. There was much concern about the safety of Jesus and these three were in charge of the security detail. Of course Sho was their main line of defense should something happen, but oftentimes what might seem like a problem with security was simply crowd control. This was a constant problem as everyone wanted to touch or be near Jesus. Sho did not like this at all and many times Jesus had to force Sho to back off from being so protective.

Finally, Jesus chose Judas Iscariot to be in charge of the group's finances. Securing money wasn't a daily task, but it was important nevertheless. Almost always when Jesus healed someone they felt obligated to either let the group stay in their home, or feed them, or give an offering of money. Anytime the gift was money it would go to Judas as he seemed to have a gift for saving money.

They arrived at the country of the Gadarenes, which is opposite Galilee. When Jesus stepped ashore, a certain man out of the city who had demons for a long time met him. He wore no clothes, and didn't live in a house, but in the tombs.

When he saw Jesus, he cried out, and fell down before him, and with a loud voice said, "What do I have to do with you, Jesus, you Son of the Most High God? I beg you, don't torment me!" For Jesus was commanding the unclean spirit to come out of the man. For the unclean spirit had often seized the man. He was kept under guard, and bound with chains and fetters. Breaking the bands apart, he was driven by the demon into the desert.

*Jesus asked him, "**What is your name?**" He said, "Legion," for many demons had entered into him. (Luke 8:26-30)*

Chapter 11

Legion

Gerasenes was a tiny village, much like Nazareth, that stood on the eastern shore of the Sea of Galilee. It had a population of fewer than one hundred people, but it did have a nice harbor that provided shelter from the fierce western winds. Jesus was working his way around the entire lake as he was beginning his ministry; Gerasenes was simply a natural layover.

Moments after Jesus stepped ashore he was met by a much troubled man, infested with demons.

As Jesus drove the demons from the man who approached him, they begged Jesus not to condemn them into the abyss. *Now there was a herd of many pigs feeding on the mountain, and they begged him that he would allow them to enter into those. He allowed them. The demons came out from the man*

*and entered into the pigs, and the herd rushed down
the steep bank into the lake, and were drowned.*

Whether by pure instinct or a command sent tele-
pathically by Jesus, Sho made a dash across a field to
a hillside where hundreds of pigs were feeding. The
pigs quickly formed a tight defensive circle as Sho
was wildly barking and gnashing his teeth at them.

A couple of men were overlooking and tending
the herd, and at this point they were amused at the dog
seeking to have its way with the group of pigs. These
were pigs, not sheep, and there was no way a dog
could herd pigs to do its will, the men were thinking.

It was at this point Sho called upon hundreds of
years of instinct and his training with the shepherds
in his youth while in Bethlehem. Because Sho's
father was a shepherd dog, Sho naturally had the
instinct to herd most anything. However his limited
experience in herding sheep in his youth kicked in
and Sho let it be known to the pigs he was in control, and they responded by forming an even tighter
circle for safety. But even in a large group as this
they were no match for the resolve of Sho and he
rushed the herd down a steep bank into the lake and
the herd drowned.

*When those who were tending them saw what
had happened, they fled and told the story in the*

city and in the country. People went out to see what had happened. They came to Jesus, and found the man from whom the demons had gone out, sitting at Jesus's feet, clothed and in his right mind; and they were afraid. Those who saw it told them how he who had been possessed by demons was healed. All the people of the surrounding country of the Gadarenes asked him to depart from them, for they were very much afraid. He entered the boat and returned.

Sho became very, very sick that night as the odor from all the demons was too much for his overdeveloped sense of smell. He was successful in driving the possessed pigs into the lake where they drowned, but each demon that left a pig tried with all its might to possess Sho. Each demon personally took it upon itself to enter Sho's body and possess his soul and with each attempted possession the demons inflicted Sho with a horrendous body blow as they tried to enter his body through his nostrils. Dozens of times Sho was knocked off his feet, but each time Sho rebounded and was able to fend off their attacks. Quickly they found out that Sho was unique in the entire animal kingdom. God had, since the incident with the Holy Spirit on the Jordan River, encircled Sho with a protective force that no man or demon or animal could penetrate. God would, at the insistence of Jesus, remove that protective force only once, but this would be a couple of years in the future.

So the Legion of demons left the area in the knowledge that Jesus and Sho were too powerful. They shot out across the lake and their shrieks could be heard for miles across the Sea of Galilee. Some say even today when the wind is blowing in from Gerasenes and you listen carefully, you can still hear the shrieks of the misplaced demons echoing across the Sea of Galilee.

However, Sho was now close to death after all the body blows the demons had inflicted. Jesus took the boat a couple of miles north of town and pulled up to shore. He jumped out of the boat and gently lifted Sho into his arms, carrying him into the hills above the town. There he found a large shade tree and carefully laid Sho on a pile of soft green grass. His breathing was now shallow and Sho was barely clinging to life. Jesus ever so calmly took Sho's snout in his hands, making certain his mouth was closed. Then Jesus took the deepest breath he had ever taken and put his mouth over the nostrils of Sho and exhaled to the bottom of his lungs. He repeated this two more times. Then, after the third breath Sho bounced up, eyes sparkling and, most important his tail wagging again. Then Jesus knew his friend would be all right. This time Jesus returned the favor and saved the life of his best friend.

I am so lucky to have Jesus as my master, Sho thought to himself. He gave Jesus a big lick on the face then lay down to take a short nap. As it happened, Sho wouldn't wake up until the next day. The following day, as Jesus was feeling very badly that the farmers had lost all of their pigs, he returned to the town and paid them for their losses. Jesus still had some of the gold left from Sho winning the race in Egypt some twenty five years earlier and used this several times during his life to help out other people who were in need.

Within two days the story of Jesus, the demons, the pigs and Sho spread to Jerusalem, increasing the legacy of Jesus. Attention was now being paid to Jesus by the ruling religious and political elites as they were trying to figure out who this Jesus really was.

But Jesus went to the Mount of Olives. Now very early in the morning, he came again into the temple, and all the people came to him. He sat down, and taught them. The scribes and the Pharisees brought a woman taken in adultery. Having set her in the midst, they told him, "Teacher, we found this woman in adultery, in the very act. Now in our law, Moses commanded us to stone such. What then do you say about her?" They said this testing him, that they might have something to accuse him of. (John 8:1-6)

Chapter 12

Jesus Meets Mary M.

J esus once again found himself within the Temple walls, teaching of the new world to come. And true to their pattern since Jesus began his ministry, the Pharisees were trying to trap him. A group of Pharisees brought a young woman caught in the act of adultery, which was a sin that was punishable by death. The Pharisees threw the woman toward Jesus and quickly formed a large circle around them. Then each began to pick up a stone as if to begin the stoning process right away.

This set Sho on high alert. Here they go again, he thought. What was it with these people that they were always tossing stones at others, trying to kill them? Sho believed they were preparing to attack Jesus, not the woman, so he immediately got into his famous "death pose." This was a straightening of his tail. Then he would arch his back and the silver-white hairs on his back would stand on edge. This would be followed by the curling of his lips so his foes could see his massive canines. And lastly he would issue a growl so deep it would cause a lion to pause.

Everyone in the land was quite aware of what Sho could do to people or animals, and, therefore no one was anxious to toss the first stone. So they backed off, but no one dropped their stone. Sho was walking the perimeter of the circle, seemingly daring someone to toss the first stone.

Then Jesus crouched to the ground, placed his finger in the dirt and began writing something. As the Pharisees kept probing Jesus as to what should be done with the adulterous woman, he stood and said to them, *"He who is without sin among you, let him throw the first stone at her."*

One by one after reflecting on what Jesus had just said, they dropped their stones and left. Either the men were afraid of Sho attacking them or deep down they knew Jesus was right. Jesus had once again evaded their trap. The Romans didn't allow the Jews to carry out death sentences so this could have been the "perfect trap." If Jesus said go ahead and stone her, this would be a conflict with the Romans. On the other hand, had he said not to stone her, this would be in conflict with Jewish law. The Pharisees thought they had Jesus in a lose-lose situation. However, once again the mind of Jesus was too great for them and he came up with the ultimate answer.

Jesus, now alone with the woman, realized she was possessed with demons. Without anyone present, without trying to teach or prove a point to anyone, he firmly touched her trembling body and immediately seven demons left her body.

Sho could smell the acrid scent and barked loudly at each of the demons as they vacated the woman's body.

After this Jesus looked around and asked her, ***"Woman, where are your accusers? Did no one condemn you?"*** She said, *"No one, Lord."* Jesus said***, "Neither do I condemn you."***

The woman began sobbing, knowing her life had been spared, plus she could feel a huge weight had been lifted from her soul when the demons left her body. She took a deep breath as if it was her first breath since being born. Then she bowed down and kissed the feet of Jesus. Jesus immediately bent down and kissed her on the forehead and said to her, ***"Go your way. From now on, sin no more."***

They went their separate ways, never guessing they would meet again, and this is how Jesus first met Mary Magdalene.

Mary's life would never be the same after this incident. She had been literally touched by God and God had spared her life. Mary, the young, attractive daughter of a wealthy businessman, now decided there must be more to life than surrounding herself with expensive things and clothes and leading a life of sin. God had spared her for a reason and she now sought out that reason. After several weeks of fighting with herself about what to do with her life, she decided to go to Galilee where she had heard Jesus was preaching and baptizing.

On a beautiful spring day, on a hillside overlooking the Sea of Galilee, she arrived just in time to hear Jesus preaching to the people. There stood Jesus on top of a huge boulder overlooking the thousands in attendance. Then he began to speak in a loud, but calm voice:

"Blessed are the poor in spirit, for theirs is the kingdom of heaven.

Blessed are those who mourn, for they will be comforted.

Blessed are the gentle, for they will inherit the earth.

Blessed are those who hunger and thirst after righteousness, for they will be filled.

Blessed are the merciful, for they shall obtain mercy.

Blessed are the pure in heart, for they will see God. Blessed are the peacemakers, for they shall be called children of God.

Blessed are those who are persecuted because of righteousness, for theirs is the kingdom of heaven. Blessed are you when people reproach you, persecute you, and say all kinds of evil against you falsely, for my sake. Rejoice, and be exceedingly glad, for great is your reward in heaven. For that is how they persecuted the prophets who were before you."

Jesus was now preaching his famous Sermon on the Mount.

Instantly Mary knew when she heard these words of Jesus that he spoke of a raw truth she had never heard from anyone. She, just like the multitudes that also heard him teach that day, was mesmerized. Truly this was a son of Israel, a prophet, but much more, Mary said to herself. Then Mary, in a crowd of thousands, made the individual choice and took the leap of faith and became a believer. Her life would never be the same. Her mind was spinning as she listened to the words of Jesus. No man had ever spoken words like these and meant them, she thought.

Jesus had been preaching nonstop to the people for hours and let the time get by him. Suddenly he noticed Sho was nowhere near him. This was very unusual as Sho almost never left his side. When Jesus realized Sho was missing, he quickly finished his Sermon on the Mount and began looking for his best friend. In a panic he called all the disciples to spread out among the crowd and find him.

Finally after many anxious minutes, Peter called out, "Look Master, down at the lake." Down on a sandy stretch of beach was Sho running back and forth, barking and playing with someone. But who was this playing with his Sho? Jesus thought. As Jesus drew closer, he realized it was a woman tossing a stick into the lake for Sho. Playing fetch in the water was his favorite game. Sho loved this game, but it also served a purpose of cooling his body down from his heavy fur. Jesus knew this wasn't like Sho to pick up with a stranger and play. But secretly he was quite pleased to see this. He had long realized since he began his ministry that his relationship with Sho had suffered. The bond between the two would never suffer— but the day-today, hour-to-hour attention Sho had received for years just wasn't there any longer. Jesus just couldn't get away from the crowds of people. His only escape was to board a boat and get some repose out on the lake.

Then, walking alone up to the woman, he realized this was the woman he met several weeks ago in Jerusalem and saved from the stoning. Before Jesus could say anything, Mary introduced herself. "My name is Mary from Magdala. You saved my life in Jerusalem and I am here to give it back to you in return", she said.

"You know he (pointing at Sho) doesn't just take up with anyone. You must be very special indeed to be making him so happy. I would consider it an honor to have you as part of my disciples. But you must know my disciples are all men and you will have to prove yourself to them," Jesus said.

Mary was young, attractive and had a million-dollar smile. "I don't think that will be a problem," she said with confidence. Then Jesus and Mary and Sho slowly walked up the hillside from the lake laughing and playing together. The disciples were shocked to see Jesus this way, but all were happy for him. From that moment Mary of Magdala became one of the guys, the thirteenth disciple—but much more.

Now when Jesus heard that John was delivered up, he withdrew into Galilee. Leaving Nazareth, he came and lived in Capernaum, which is by the sea, in the region of Zebulun and Naphtali, that it might be fulfilled which was spoken through Isaiah the prophet, saying,

"The land of Zebulun and the land of Naphtali,
Toward the sea, beyond the Jordan, Galilee of the Gentiles,
The people who sat in darkness saw a great light,
To those who sat in the region and shadow of death,
To them light has dawned." (Matthew 4:12-16)

Chapter 13

University of Capernaum

After the debacle in Nazareth, Jesus decided he needed a new home, a new base of operations for his ministry. He didn't go out immediately seeking a new headquarters, but traveled the Galilean countryside for a time, preaching and healing. There had never been anyone like Jesus in all of Jewish history. Surely John was a prophet but he never healed people, cast out demons, or ever performed miracles as did Jesus. Jesus did not quote human authorities as did the "teachers" of the law, but used the authority directly from God. There was no middleman here. The people were amazed at this. Everyone could readily see this was something new and different, including the Jewish authorities in Jerusalem.

For the greater part of his ministry Jesus had no home; he simply traveled the area. Every so often the band would travel up to Capernaum and while there, stay in the house of Peter and Andrew. This worked out well for all as Capernaum was a quaint town directly on the western shore of the Sea of Galilee. It was on an ancient highway that went from the coast of the Mediterranean Sea to Damascus. It had a sizeable two-story synagogue crafted from limestone, which was the centerpiece structure in town. This was a perfect place to call his headquarters and the town had a good mix of Jews and Gentiles.

As far as Sho was concerned, Capernaum was his favorite town. Being right on the lake, Sho could wander freely up and down the shoreline and always find adventure. There were lots of fishermen who would go out of their way to make certain Sho was given a fresh fish. Just as Sho was a favorite among the shepherds (many times over the years Sho was called upon to rid flocks of killer wolves), he was also loved by the local fishermen. Oftentimes Sho would jump into the lake, knowing where fishermen had their nets placed, and drive schools of fish straight into them. Sho was an excellent swimmer as he had learned to swim as a young dog on his fishing trips with Jesus. Oftentimes some of the fishermen who knew Peter or Andrew well would come and ask

Jesus for permission to borrow Sho to help with their fishing. Jesus was always more than happy to loan him out, as he knew how happy it made Sho to get in the cool, clean water of the lake.

The synagogue was a place where Jews could study the Scriptures and worship God. The synagogue originated during the Jewish exile and was very important in keeping the people connected with God. A synagogue could be established in any town where there were at least ten married Jewish men. Therefore almost any village, regardless of size, had its own synagogue.

Capernaum was a beautiful city located right on the waters of the Sea of Galilee. The lake itself was below sea level and fed by the cold, clear waters of the Jordan River. Capernaum was on the northernmost part of the lake. Capernaum was an odd mix of Jews, Romans and Greeks.

This would be a perfect place to spread the "new" word of God to the people, Jesus thought, and it would also be a central location where the people could come to him.

And come they did.

In the synagogue there was a man who had a spirit of an unclean demon and he cried out with a loud voice, saying, *"Ah! What have we to do with you Jesus of Nazareth? Have you come to destroy us? I know you who you are: the Holy One of God!"*

Jesus rebuked him, saying, **"Be silent and come out of him!"** When the demon had thrown him down in their midst, he came out of him, having done him no harm.

Amazement came on all, and they spoke together, one with another, saying, *"What is this word? For with authority and power he commands the unclean spirits, and they come out!"* News about him went out into every place of the surrounding region.

Sho always found it quite interesting when Jesus drove an evil spirit from a person, as he could detect a rank odor coming forth from the person. Humans didn't seem to pick up on this, but it always smelled like a dead animal. The smell would seem to hover over the person for several seconds then vanish. Demons were all very odd, Sho thought to himself.

Sho had a special place designated for him in the synagogue. It was atop a large alabaster altar that overlooked the congregation. Sho liked this spot for he could look into the eyes of each of the men in the crowd. He would sit atop the altar, as motionless as the piece of stone he was on, scanning the crowd for trouble; all the while wrinkling his nose sniffing for trouble. Jesus took great pleasure watching Sho take his responsibilities of security so seriously.

Sho would usually smell trouble before it happened. It was a given that in every crowd there were spies planted by the Sanhedrin to inform them of what Jesus was up to. Sho could smell them a mile away and would often walk up to them and raise his leg and relieve himself on them and Jesus never intervened when Sho did this! Whenever this would happen, the crowd would burst into laughter as they did not care for the religious aristocracy from Jerusalem anyway.

While in Capernaum, a Roman centurion with one hundred men under his command had a valued servant become deathly ill. Death for the servant was hours away and leaders in the Jewish community went to Jesus to try to sway him to help the centurion. They said to Jesus, *"He is worthy for you to do this for him, for he loves our nation and he built our synagogue for us."* Jesus decided to go with them. As Jesus was not far from the home, the centurion sent friends to Jesus and gave him this message: *"Lord, don't trouble yourself, for I am not worthy for you to come under my roof. Therefore I didn't even think myself worthy to come to you; but say the word, and my servant will be healed. For I also am a man placed under authority, having under myself soldiers. I tell this one, 'Go!' and he goes; and to another, 'Come!' and he comes; and to my servant, 'Do this', and he does it."*

When Jesus heard these things, he marveled at him and turned and said to the multitude who followed him, **"I tell you, I have not found such great faith, no, not in Israel."** Those who were sent, returning to the house, found that the servant who had been sick was well.

From that time on Jesus had the full support from the Romans and the Jews, at least in Capernaum.

For Herod had laid hold of John, and bound him, and put him in prison for the sake of Herodias, his brother Philip's wife. For John said to him, "It is not lawful for you to have her." When he would have put him to death, he feared the multitude, because they counted him as a prophet.

But when Herod's birthday came, the daughter of Herodias danced among them and pleased Herod. Whereupon he promised with an oath to give her whatever she should ask. She, being prompted by her mother, said, "Give me here on a platter the head of the John the Baptizer."

The king was grieved, but for the sake of his oaths, and of those who sat at the table with him, he commanded it to be given, and he sent and beheaded John in the prison. His head was brought on a platter, and given to the young lady: and she brought it to her mother.

His disciples came, and took the body, and buried it; and they went and told Jesus. (Matthew 14:3-12)

Chapter 14

Walking on Water

Everyone was in shock at the news of John. The people knew Herod to be a despot, but taking the life of the Baptist was crossing the line. John truly was a prophet who walked with God and the people knew this. Jesus, of course, had lost a boyhood friend and family member. The pain Jesus felt was the sharpest he had felt since he learned about the death of Joseph. He was now feeling the same pain and it made him weep and grieve.

Sho was very sad to see Jesus in this state of mind. The best thing he could do he, thought, was simply sit next to his friend and Master in his hour of need. Jesus held on to Sho as the tears kept flowing. Sho would help Jesus get through this, whatever it would take! How could the cruelty of man toward man be any more manifest than taking the life of an innocent like John? Jesus thought.

Jesus withdrew to a deserted place to contemplate the future and his ministry. But the people were in shock learning of the news of their beloved John and came from cities all around, seeking Jesus out.

Jesus went out and he saw a great multitude. He had compassion on them and healed their sick. When evening had come, his disciples came to him, saying, "This place is deserted, and the hour is already late. Send the multitudes away, that they may go into the villages, and buy themselves food."

But Jesus said to them, **"They don't need to go away. You give them something to eat."**

They told him, *"We only have here five loaves and two fish."*

He said, **"Bring them here to me."**

He commanded the multitudes to sit down on the grass; and he took the five loaves and the two fish, and looking up to heaven, he blessed, broke and gave the loaves to the disciples, and the disciples gave to the multitudes. They all ate, and were filled. They took up twelve baskets full of that which remained left over from the broken pieces. Those who ate were about five thousand men, besides women and children.

Sho thought to himself, "This is a lot of fun." People were running around acting like children as they witnessed Jesus perform this miracle. For Sho it meant plenty of food, the procurement of which was often a challenge for him. Many times he would go to sleep hungry, but somehow Jesus always made certain he had enough. But he was now at his peak and weighed around one hundred ten pounds, so it took a lot of calories to satisfy his big frame. People from all over the region were here, still in shock wondering what they would do without the Baptist in their world.

Jesus continued healing the sick and giving words of comfort to the crowd, although it was difficult emotionally for him to keep his composure. But he found helping the people kept his mind away from the bad news of John. Jesus had the disciples get into a boat that was nearby. He felt it would be good for Sho to go along with the disciples as they, too, were visibly upset concerning the news of John. Would they and Jesus be next? many of them were thinking to themselves. Anyway, Jesus thought, it would be a great way for them to get to know Sho a little better and it would also be a way for Sho to learn something about each of them. As they cast off in the boat, Jesus separated himself from the crowd and went up into the hills to pray.

But the boat was now in the middle of the sea, distressed by the waves, for the wind was contrary.

In the fourth watch [about 3 am] of the night, Jesus came to them, walking on the sea. When the disciples saw him walking on the sea, they were troubled, saying, "It's a ghost!" and they cried out for fear. But immediately Jesus spoke to them, saying, **"Cheer up! It is I! Don't be afraid."**

Peter answered him and said, "Lord if it is you, command me to come to you on the waters."

He said, **"Come!"**

When Sho heard the command "come" from Jesus he immediately, without thinking, jumped from the boat and skipped over the surface of the water toward Jesus some fifty feet away. Jesus whistled in his special shrill they had perfected over the years and Sho glided over the top of the water as if he had wings, then about five feet from Jesus he leapt into his outstretched arms. The disciples could not believe their eyes at what they had just witnessed. Seeing this...

Peter stepped down from the boat, and walked on the waters to come to Jesus. But when he saw that the wind was strong, he was afraid, and beginning to sink, he cried out, saying, "Lord, save me!"

Immediately Jesus, holding on to Sho with one hand, stretched out his other hand, took hold of

Peter, and said to him, *"You of little faith, why did you doubt?"*

When they got up into the boat, the wind ceased. Those who were in the boat came and worshiped him, saying, "You are truly the Son of God!"

Jesus shook his head and admonished his disciples and said, **"How is it the faith of a dog can exceed the faith of a man?"** And Jesus was disappointed in the twelve, but he was never as proud of Sho as he was at that moment. Sho had shown them, through action, what the power of the mind and an unbridled faith can achieve. Jesus put his arms around the dry coat of Sho and pointed at the water-soaked Peter and burst into laughter. Almost immediately the rest joined Jesus and began poking fun at Peter, each disciple secretly glad it was not he whom Jesus was having fun with.

Going on from that place, he went into their synagogue, and a man with a shriveled hand was there. Looking for a reason to bring charges against Jesus, they asked him, "Is it lawful to heal on the Sabbath?"

*He said to them, **"If any of you has a sheep and it falls into a pit on the Sabbath, will you not take hold of it and lift it out? How much more valuable is a person than a sheep! Therefore it is lawful to do good on the Sabbath."** Then he said to the man, **"Stretch out your hand."** So he stretched it out and it was completely restored just as sound as the other. But the Pharisees went out and plotted how they might kill Jesus. (Matthew 12:9-14)*

Chapter 15

The Assassination Attempt

J esus did not know it at the time, but his life was now in grave danger. He was no threat to Rome—yet. He was no threat to Herod—yet. However, he was becoming a serious threat in the eyes of the ruling religious elites of the day—the Sanhedrin.

The Sanhedrin was the supreme Jewish political, religious and judicial body of its day. It was composed of seventy members. The group fell under two religious camps: the Pharisees and the Sadducees. The Pharisees were in charge of teaching the Law of Moses to the people. The Sadducees were the priestly leaders of the temple. The Sanhedrin would meet daily, but never on Sabbaths or Holy Days. The Sanhedrin was overseen by a high priest whose name was Joseph Caiaphas. The Romans considered the high priest to be the person responsible for Jewish concerns in Jerusalem and any issue the Romans had would end up on the lap of Caiaphas. He would do anything to maintain the status quo in Jerusalem and it was very obvious to him that Jesus had to be eliminated.

Jesus had been ministering around the Galilee for some two years. The "inner circle" of the Sanhedrin met in secret and decided the teachings of Jesus were too much of a threat to their rule and Jesus must be removed from the scene. Since they had no law to put a man to death, they would hire assassins to do their dirty work. They had done this before, a couple of times over the years.

So they put out a contract on the life of Jesus. They had to be very careful, however. Jesus was very popular with the people and any link back to the Sanhedrin would be devastating. So it was decided they would procure the services of the secret group known only as the Tartan Zealots. Little was known about this secret group except they were known never to have failed on a mission. For centuries they had been doing the dirty work of Roman emperors, Egyptian kings, rich trade merchants, slave traders and anyone else who had enough money, including the Sanhedrin.

No one in the Sanhedrin had ever had direct contact with the Tartans, but they were generally known to be in the vicinity of Mount Ararat, protected from all sides by the walls of the mountain. So the Sanhedrin sent an emissary with fifty talents of gold to have Jesus killed. This was a lot of money, but on the other hand it was only about a month's worth of offerings by the people at the Temple. This would be money well spent. For if Jesus kept on like this, there would be no more Temple priests—they would all be out of power.

A couple of months after the incident in the grain field, Jesus decided to return to Capernaum.

He entered into a boat and crossed over, and came into his own city. Behold, they brought to him a man who was paralyzed, lying on a bed. Jesus, seeing their faith, said to the paralytic, **"Son, cheer up! Your sins are forgiven you."** *Behold, some of the scribes said to themselves, "This man blasphemes."* Again Jesus was forgiving the sins of a man and in the minds of the Jewish leaders, only God could forgive sins!

Hidden in the crowd were the four assassins hired by the Sanhedrin. They blended in well as the crowds now following Jesus were quite large with people from many diverse areas. It was decided that tonight would be the time to strike. The leaders of the Sanhedrin wanted Jesus to die in his adopted hometown far away from the mobs of Jerusalem where news of this sort could upset the people. Also in the crowd were a couple of Pharisees from the Sanhedrin who wanted to make certain the job got done and the contract completed. No more Jesus after tonight, they thought.

That evening a feast was given to Jesus by the townspeople. There was much wine flowing, dancing, singing and lots of food. Jesus was happy being back in his adopted hometown of Capernaum and being shown so much love and appreciation.

A feast always got Sho excited. He had long ago figured out that when there was a large group of humans having fun, there was lots of food to be had. Sho got his fill of meat as everyone considered it an honor to personally feed the dog of Jesus. He was all too happy to accommodate them. He had so much meat he had to excuse himself from the party, go outside and vomit. But it was all right; he had not eaten like this in months.

Jesus decided earlier that day he wanted to sleep with his disciples in some gardens high on a hilltop that overlooked Capernaum and the Sea of Galilee.

Tonight he would not be sleeping at the family home of Peter.

After the party broke up, Sho, Jesus and his disciples made their way to the beautiful gardens. There were groves of olive trees and of course Jesus's favorite—figs. Following in the darkness were the assassins. They would strike tonight. Armed with knives only, their plan was to slit the throat of Jesus when he was sleeping. A quick in, and, out and no one, including his disciples, would know a thing. For the Assassins of Tartan had never been seen, at least by anyone who had lived to tell about it. From the age of five all boys were trained in the art of killing and only one in ten boys ever made it to graduation, which would be at the age of eighteen. So these men were the best of the best and had no weaknesses.

As Jesus and his disciples each staked out a place to unroll their sleeping blankets, Jesus recounted the story of how years earlier the cobra had tried to kill him in his youth. The disciples were always in awe of Sho anyway, but after that story, they felt more reverence toward Sho than awe. Jesus then said a group prayer for all and they lay down for the night. Most were asleep within seconds as they had way too much wine and food and were exhausted from the day's events.

Sho took his usual spot next to Jesus. Jesus fell asleep quickly as well. Sho also closed his eyes and dreamt of the cobra that had taken his life years earlier. This field reminded Jesus and Sho of their family food plot back in Nazareth. It was a peaceful evening and the only sound to be heard was the crackling of their campfire.

It was now late night and the only things moving were the stars on their nightly path. Sho woke up and scanned the camp to make certain all was well. He detected no problems and moved to the other side of Jesus as was his custom. Within seconds Sho was fast asleep.

Then something remarkable happened: Sho was awakened by his nose. His keen sense of smell detected danger, extreme danger. Even though he was in a deep sleep his nose woke him up. He barely opened his eyes and he could see shadows moving in the dark. It appeared there were four moving shadows coming toward the sleeping Jesus. Is this a dream? he thought. Then before he could even process what was happening, two of the shadow men yielding knives lunged at Jesus. Sho shot up and intercepted the two, slashing their throats in midair. All this happened within two seconds. Before their bodies hit the ground, the other two made their way toward Jesus.

Everyone was awake now, including Jesus. Sho was now standing between them and Jesus. They were trying to get past Sho, but could not. What they did not know was that Sho was never defense-minded. He always acted first and won his battles in large part because of this. While the remaining assassins were trying to figure out how to get to Jesus, Sho leapt into the air and ripped apart the face of one of them; and he collapsed to the ground, dying within a couple of minutes. Now with just one shadow man left, Sho was ready to complete the job. Just as Sho was about to finish off the last assassin Jesus shouted, **"Sho stop!"**

Immediately Sho froze, tail erect, ears at attention, his body still in a death posture ready at a moment's command. The twelve could not believe their eyes. Their master was within moments of being killed. Killed by whom and why? Who would want Jesus dead?

Now the remaining assassin was surrounded by the twelve, some of whom carried knives of their own. Jesus, with Sho standing directly in front of him, asked the man where he was from and why they tried to kill him. But before they could get any information from him he quickly put his knife to his throat and sliced it open. The man dropped to the ground and died. Shaken, Jesus walked Sho to a nearby brook and washed away the blood stains from coat of Sho, returning it to its state of pristine white.

That morning Jesus and the twelve gathered the four bodies and brought them into Capernaum. Within minutes the entire village was surrounding the bodies wondering what had happened. With everyone in the village present, Jesus looked up and saw two Pharisees talking with one another in a panic. Jesus then figured out the plot and scolded them. **"Go to the Sanhedrin and tell them what you have seen here. For the Father protects his sheep and his shepherd,"** Jesus said. With that the Sanhedrin withdrew the contract on the life of Jesus for fear it would get out into the public what they had intended.

It was the Feast of the Dedication at Jerusalem. It was winter, and Jesus was walking in the temple, in Solomon's porch. The Jews therefore came around him and said to him, "How long will you hold us in suspense? If you are the Christ, tell us plainly."

Jesus answered them, "I told you, and you don't believe. The works that I do in my Father's name, these testify about me. But you don't believe, because you are not of my sheep, as I told you. My sheep hear my voice, and I know them, and they follow me. I give eternal life to them, they will never perish, and no one will snatch them out of my hand. My Father, who has given them to me, is greater than all. No one is able to snatch them out of my Father's hand. I and the Father are one." (John 10:22-30)

Chapter 16

Jews and Stones

It was a bright, sunny winter day during the holy week known as Hanukkah. Jesus, his disciples and Sho were walking the Temple grounds and came upon the area known as Solomon's Colonnade. This area was built by Herod when he restored the temple. It was a large, open area and became over time a general gathering area used by the people.

As usual, it did not take Jesus very long to attract a crowd. This group mostly consisted of Pharisees who had just left their private meeting area after morning prayers. One of the men in the group, trying to trap Jesus into saying something that could get him arrested or killed, asked the following: *"If you are the Christ, tell us plainly."*

Jesus repeated himself and said, **"I and the Father are one."**

Therefore Jews took up stones again to stone him. Jesus answered them, *"I have shown you many good works from my Father. For which of those works do you stone me?"*

No sooner had Jesus said this to the Pharisees than Sho sprang into action. Seeing strangers pick up stones immediately brought him back to the episode when Jesus was a boy and the group of kids tried to hurt Jesus by stoning him. Within a split second Sho was in front of Jesus, tail straight, eyes fixated on the person who was talking, and Sho curled his upper lip so he could easily see his razor teeth which were glistening in the sun. This one, he thought, would be the first one he would kill if a single stone was tossed towards Jesus.

This group of the Sanhedrin was fully aware of the damage Sho could inflict. They knew firsthand that Sho had killed three of the assassins who had gone after Jesus earlier that year. After all, they were the ones who had hired the foursome to do their dirty work.

Sho walked in a tight circle around Jesus, scanning the crowd, waiting for any movement that looked threatening. As Sho kept pacing, Jesus was talking to the people, looking to teach them more about their God. One of the Pharisees blurted out, *"We* don't stone you for a good work, but for blasphemy: because you, being a man, make yourself God."

Jesus answered them, *"Isn't it written in your law, I said, you are gods, to whom the word of God came (and the Scripture can't be broken), do you say of him whom the Father sanctified and sent into the world, 'You blaspheme,' because I said, 'I am the Son of God?' If I don't do the works of my Father, don't believe me. But if I do them, though you don't believe me, believe the works; that you may know and believe that the Father is in me, and I in the Father."*

Each of the Jews threw down the rocks they were ready to use as weapons against Jesus. It was simply a choice of trying to stone Jesus right there on the Temple grounds and risk being killed by Sho or walk away and find another way. Not one man had the courage to face Sho. So they turned their backs on Jesus and left in frustration. Meanwhile Jesus was mobbed by the people to learn more.

However, it was becoming clearer to Jesus that the Jewish religious leaders wanted to eliminate him rather than embrace the message he was bringing them. So Jesus and his disciples (and of course Sho) went back to the Jordan, in the general area where John had been baptizing. This was much more to

Jesus's liking as he did not care for large cities. Cities held too many dishonorable people hiding behind shadows, he thought. Jesus loved the open air and the simplicity of country living. Plus he always felt Sho was happier in the country, where he could chase game and play in the river. In addition, Sho always felt it was easier for him to guard Jesus out in the open, where he could better use his keen senses.

That evening before the journey to the Jordan, one of the Pharisees named Nicodemus, who was a ruler of the Jews, came to visit Jesus. He did this at night so as not to be seen by his peers. Nicodemus said to Jesus, *"Rabbi, we know that you are a teacher come from God, for no one can do these signs that you do unless God is with him."*

Jesus said, *"Most certainly, I tell you, unless one is born anew, he can't see the Kingdom of God."*

Nicodemus said to him, *"How can a man be born when he is old? Can he enter a second time into his mother's womb, and be born?"*

Jesus answered, *"Most certainly I tell you, unless one is born of water and spirit, he can't enter into the Kingdom of God! That which is born of the flesh is flesh. That which is born of the Spirit is spirit. Don't marvel that I said to you, 'You must be*

born anew.' The wind blows going. So is everyone
who is born of the Spirit."

Nicodemus answered him, *"How can these
things be?"*

Jesus answered him, **"Are you the teacher of
Israel, and don't understand these things? As Moses
lifted up the serpent in the wilderness, even so must
the Son of Man be lifted up, that whoever believes
in him should not perish, but have eternal life. For
God so loved the world, that he gave his one and
only Son, that whoever believes in him should not
perish, but have eternal life."**

With that Nicodemus looked dumbfounded and
bade Jesus a good evening. But Nicodemus would
never have a good night's sleep after this encounter
with Jesus and was haunted with nightmares the
remainder of his life. He could never reconcile the
ghost of Moses with the Spirit of Jesus.

Now a man named Lazarus was sick. He was from Bethany, the village of Mary and her sister Martha. (This Mary, whose brother Lazarus now lay sick, was the same one who poured perfume on the Lord and wiped his feet with her hair.) So the sisters sent word to Jesus, "Lord, the one you love is sick."

When he heard this, Jesus said, **"This sickness will not end in death. No, it is for God's glory so that God's Son may be glorified through it."** *Now Jesus loved Martha and her sister and Lazarus. So when he heard that Lazarus was sick, he stayed where he was two more days, and then he said to his disciples,* **"Let us go back to Judea."** *"But Rabbi," they said, "a short while ago the Jews there tried to stone you, and yet you are going back?" (John 11:1-8)*

Chapter 17

The Death of Lazarus

J esus knew a return trip to Jerusalem would be a risky proposition. After the assassination attempt and the religious leaders threatening to stone him in the Temple courtyard, a return could turn into a complete disaster. Things needed to cool off, but the sudden news of the sickness of his old friend Lazarus called for his immediate attention.

Jesus met with his disciples and let them know a return to Jerusalem (Bethany) was imminent. This was news none of the disciples wanted to hear. All were worried not only of their fates, but of Jesus as well. That evening as they sat around the campfire on the bank of the Jordan River, you could feel the tension as barely a word was spoken. Jesus, sensing that a bit of fun was in order to take away their anguish started a little game with his disciples and Sho.

Sho's favorite treat was a concoction of dates, barley and sesame seeds. Whenever Jesus had the ingredients available, he would either make them himself for Sho or have someone else do it. So that early-spring evening as they formed a circle around a blazing fire overlooking the Jordan, Jesus set out to play a game with Sho and his disciples. Jesus, without even getting up, would place a treat on the person of one of the disciples and Sho had to figure out which disciple had the treat. Sho would calmly walk around the group with his nose inhaling whiffs of air, trying to locate the scent of his favorite treat and who might be holding the prize.

There was Sho, trying to get the occasional whiff of the faintest of molecules of his favorite treat; this was not easy as the smoke from the fire masked the odor. Jesus got a big laugh seeing his best friend try to figure out which person held the prize. Everyone burst into laughter at the sight of Sho crinkling his big black nose, trying to filter out the smoke from the fire and homing in on the prize.

The most difficult treat to find was on the person of Judas. Sho calmly walked up to Judas and sniffed him from head to toe. Judas was a little uneasy, as he was certain Sho did not like him anyway. After giving up on the idea that Judas held the prize, Sho walked around the circle once more and again found his way back to Judas. Then Sho stiffened his tail and let out a loud bark and stuck his muzzle in the brown leather satchel Judas kept close by his side at all times. The satchel was where Judas kept the group's pool of money. It never was much money, but enough to cover some basic expenses the group had. Sure enough, Judas opened up the satchel and there was the treat. Judas was amazed, as Jesus had never left his feet to place the treat in the bag.

Jesus repeated this for over an hour as the group and Sho kept guessing where the treat would be. Everyone broke into a loud laugh whenever Sho claimed the prize. Finally, with his belly stuffed with date treats, Sho lay down next to Jesus and let out a loud moan. He had had enough.

The most unusual part of this evening is that was the only time any of the disciples had seen Jesus use his powers just for sheer fun. So that evening, they all went to bed knowing they had a big trip ahead of them, but only Jesus knew how big this trip would become.

The trip from their sanctuary on the Jordan to Jerusalem took approximately three days. The group walked hard without many breaks. Now Jesus always had dozens, if not hundreds of people following him wherever he went. Many dropped off from this trip, as his pace was too fast. Few people, if any, could outpace Jesus. He walked everywhere and loved it. He would completely wear through a pair of sandals in six months. For most people a pair of sandals might last several years. Jesus didn't indulge in himself for much of anything, but he always insisted in having a good pair of shoes. He had a shoemaker in Jerusalem and would always drop in whenever he was passing through to pick up a new pair. The shoe cobbler was from the Levite tribe, as they controlled almost all the leather business in Israel, and he and Jesus had become quite good friends over the years.

When Jesus arrived, he found that Lazarus had been in the tomb four days already. Bethany was near Jerusalem, about fifteen stadia [two miles] away. Many of the Jews had joined the women around Martha and Mary, to console them about their brother. Then when Martha heard that Jesus was coming, she went to meet him, but Mary stayed in the house.

There Martha said to Jesus, *"Lord, if you would have been here, my brother wouldn't have died. Even now I know that, whatever you ask of God, God will give you."* Jesus said to her, **"Your brother will rise again."** Martha said to him, *"I know that he will rise again in the resurrection at the last day."*

Jesus said to her, *"I am the resurrection and the life. He who believes in me will still live, even if he dies. Whoever lives and believes in me will never die. Do you believe this?"*

She said to him, *"Yes, Lord. I have come to believe that you are the Christ, God's Son, he who comes into the world."*

Martha then called Mary, her sister. "Jesus is calling for you," she said. When Mary got to the place where Jesus was, she fell at his feet and said, *"Lord, if you would have been here, my brother wouldn't have died."* When Jesus saw her and those who had come along with her weeping, he became so full of emotions that he also wept. People had seen Jesus laugh, sing, dance, shout and pray in public, but this was the first time he was seen crying in public. So everyone knew the extent of Jesus's feelings for Lazarus.

Mary and Martha escorted Jesus to the tomb where they had laid Lazarus days ago. Then Jesus commanded some of his disciples to remove the stone blocking the cave. Martha was very concerned, for she could smell the distinct odor of death from the tomb even with the stone covering the face of it.

Then Jesus performed his greatest miracle. As they took away the stone, Jesus looked toward the heavens and said, *"Father, I thank you that you listened to me. I know that you always listen to me, but because of the multitude that stands around I said this, that they may believe that you sent me."* When he had said this, he cried with a loud voice, *"Lazarus, come out!"*

For several minutes nothing happened. You could easily hear some people in the background laughing at Jesus behind his back. How dare he think he can raise the dead? they scoffed. This was only for God to do. Not even his disciples thought he could do this. Then, quite suddenly you could see a form wrapped in white linen come from the back of the cave, slowly toward the front. There, before everyone, stood Lazarus. A couple of the women in the crowd, including Martha, fainted as they could not believe their eyes.

Jesus said to them, "Free him, and let him go."

Everyone in the crowd was shaken by this event; even the disciples could not believe their eyes. Because no man could ever do something like this, it became clear to those present that Jesus had the blessing of God in all his powers.

Sho, who had also come back from the dead, didn't much like this scene. The stench from the dead man overpowered his keen sense of smell and it made him sick. There was no way, he thought, he was going to get close to that man and he didn't. He did, however, go over to Martha and lick her face several times, which seemed to revive her. Jesus patted him on his head and said something to Sho in a language no one knew.

In an ultimate twist of irony, the saving of Lazarus's life sealed the fate of Jesus's life. Immediately people went directly to the Sanhedrin to report the miracle they had just witnessed. Jesus was now the most popular figure in the entire land. The common people loved him and he always drew huge crowds. Not so the chief priests of the land, or any Roman. Then Caiaphas, who was the high priest, said to those in the Sanhedrin, *"You know nothing at all. You do not realize that it is better for you that one man die for the people than that the whole nation perish."*

From that moment forward, the Sanhedrin spent much of their time scheming on how to kill Jesus. Jesus immediately left Bethany, not even staying around to speak to Lazarus as he was so concerned those in Jerusalem would try to arrest him. For he knew that his time had not yet come.

When they drew near to Jerusalem, to Bethphage and Bethany, at the Mount of Olives, he sent two of his disciples and said to them,

"Go your way into the village that is opposite you. Immediately as you enter into it, you will find a young donkey tied, on which no one has sat. Untie him and bring him. If anyone asks you, 'Why are you doing this?' say, 'The Lord needs him'; and immediately he will send him back here."

They went away, and found a young donkey tied at the door outside in the open street, and they untied him. Some of those who stood there asked them, "What are you doing, untying the young donkey?" They said to them just as Jesus had said, and they let them go.

They brought the young donkey to Jesus, and threw their garments on it, and Jesus sat on it. Many spread their garments on the way, and others were cutting down branches from the trees, and spreading them on the road. Those who went in front, and those who followed, cried out, "Hosanna! Blessed is he who comes in the name of the Lord! Blessed is the kingdom of our father David that is coming in the name of the Lord! Hosanna in the highest!" (Mark 11:1-10)

Chapter 18

The Final Week

Sunday and Monday

No one, except Jesus, knew this would be his final trip to Jerusalem. His life, and his ministry would soon be coming to an end within the walls of the sacred city. How fitting it was that Jesus, riding on the back of a humble donkey, would enter Jerusalem in complete triumph. The people of Israel loved Jesus. Among the people he had no enemies. He had spent his entire ministry helping the helpless. He cured the sick, and fed the hungry, and his message of love was well received by the people. Along the way people joined him on the journey to Jerusalem for the Passover. By the time Jesus reached the outskirts of Jerusalem, the crowd was in the hundreds! For this occasion Jesus procured a new white tunic with a purple belt around his waist. It was a mixed signal seeing Jesus, the man of the people, the most popular person in all the land, entering Jerusalem on top of a donkey. No Roman would ever do this and that was, in part, the point Jesus was making.

Leading the procession into Jerusalem, of course, was Sho. He never looked as grand and stately as he cleared a path through the people for Jesus and his disciples. He kept his nose high in the air in order to detect any danger. His eyes were wide open and his ears were twitching in the wind listening for any "wrong" sounds he might hear. But it was almost impossible to hear as there were so many shouts and cheers from the people showing their love for Jesus. People were fighting one another just to get close to Jesus and possibly touch him. He had won them over the hard way, walking from village to village, one by one, for four years now. The Jewish people respected Moses, but they loved Jesus.

How striking that only a couple of hours earlier Pontius Pilate, the Roman governor of the land, had also entered the city through the same gate. Pilate was sitting high atop an Arabian horse four times the size of the humble donkey Jesus rode on. There were no people cheering for Pilate and his armed escort of Roman soldiers. No one dare try any display of protest, lest they be cut down immediately. Pilate, like everyone else, was in Jerusalem for the week of Passover, the most sacred week of the Jewish calendar. He was there to make certain the people were well-aware of the total Roman control over their lives by having a visible presence.

Both Pilate and Caiaphas witnessed this triumphant entry by Jesus. Caiaphas was alarmed. Pilate was amused. Nothing, Pilate thought, especially a so-called prophet like Jesus, could ever threaten the sovereignty of mighty Rome. Let him ride his little donkey around the streets of Jerusalem if he chooses to, he thought.

Jesus rode directly to the Temple, but it was basically empty, as it was late in the day. So Jesus made certain the young colt was returned to its owner and returned to Bethany with the twelve to retire for the evening. The group was staying with supporters, and everyone enjoyed an evening of singing and dancing. Jesus knew this could well be the last chance he would have to share time with friends and was very happy to do so.

Sho had long reached a status where he no longer had to search for a meal. People across the land considered it an honor to feed the great Shomer. Sho always had a full belly the last few years. It had gotten to a point where Jesus would often wonder if people came to see and hear him, or to get a glimpse of Sho?

That evening as they lay down for the evening, Jesus had to rub Sho's stomach, as he had eaten way too much. **"Our guests are killing you with kindness,"** he said to Sho. Sho rolled over and let out a soft moan and fell asleep, as it had been a long, long day for Jesus's friend and guard dog.

Early the next day Jesus was up before everyone else, as was his normal habit. This was his "quiet time" of day when he could meditate and pray in private. Sho had learned long ago he would not bother to get up until Jesus said to. Today, Jesus thought, would be a long day dealing with the ruling religious elites of Jerusalem.

Once the team reached Jerusalem, Jesus entered the Temple area. Immediately he began tossing out those who were using God's Temple as a profit center. Just as he had done once before, he began overturning tables of the money changers. These were people who would exchange the money brought in by pilgrims into the local currency; the annual Temple tax had to be paid in that money.

Sho remembered this place and was already on high alert. It was here he remembered that he had the confrontation with the "gladiator dogs" a couple of years ago. He could smell danger the moment they walked through the Temple gates. Sho had developed a unique skill over the years and that was the ability to go from an alert state based on defense, to an alarm state based on offense. He immediately went into an offensive mode as the smell he was detecting was death. Someone, or something, was going to die today within the Temple walls. He immediately made a dash for the steps that overlooked the patio where Jesus was rearranging things. Just as Sho thought— there they were. Only this time they looked younger and smelled differently. These were the replacement dogs, he guessed. The handlers appeared to be the same, but definitely different dogs; these were younger, stronger and now there was one more to deal with. Now he would have to contend with three.

Caiaphas and the Sanhedrin had planned this trap long ago. After the Temple incident a couple of years earlier where Jesus went after everyone, they had the idea he might return. So Caiaphas met with Pilate and paid a good sum of money to the Roman governor to procure three new dogs to guard the Temple. However, these must be dogs that had tasted human blood. These dogs must be mean to the core and kill for sport. For the rulers of the Jewish people knew how well-liked Jesus was among the common people. They loved him. Therefore, the perfect way to dispatch Jesus would be to make it look like an accident. What better way than to be mauled to death by the trio of Temple guard dogs—the perfect looking accident. The Sanhedrin could then blame out-of- control Roman dogs for killing Jesus. Perfect.

Immediately Sho followed the scent of the dogs. These dogs all had massive scars alongside their bodies from the games at the Roman Coliseum. They had all tasted blood, both human and animal. They did not like men; even their handlers were afraid of them. They were handpicked by the top gladiators in Rome to be brought to Jerusalem just for this moment.

Jesus was running around the Temple shouting about "God's house" and how the money changers were robbers. He was upending tables and money was flying everywhere. Then the twelve joined in and did the same. The scene was total confusion. Caiaphas was high above on a balcony overlooking this part of the Temple and knew this would be the time to unleash the dogs and kill Jesus. He immediately gave the order for the handlers to unleash their death dogs.

Suddenly everyone stopped what they were doing, including Jesus, and the attention turned to Sho as he was now completely encircled by the trio. Just as they had done in Rome when they killed a lion, they surrounded the animal and moved in a circular motion looking for a weakness in their prey. Somehow the dogs knew in order to get to Jesus they would have to deal with Sho first. Sho arched his back and straightened his tail. He knew he would be the first to strike. He put all the force he could into his back legs and leapt high into the air, easily clearing the jaws of two of the dogs. This happened so fast the dogs didn't realize Sho was now behind two of them. With the force of an elephant, he put his giant front paws on the back of one of the dogs and snapped his back in two. You could hear the break from the far side of the Temple.

One down, two left, he thought. Just as he had done so many years ago with the cobra that was poised to kill Jesus, Sho went airborne again and went straight for the two. In midair he slashed the throat of one of them. It happened so fast, no one, not even Jesus, could see how he could accomplish this feat. Now there was one. The remaining dog made a desperate move to try to get under Sho at his belly. One good bite there and the white dog would be dead, he thought. In a surprise move to Sho, the dog came at him in what appeared head-to- head, then at the last instant dove underneath Sho. Sho, realizing what was happening, did a complete three-sixty summersault, now exposing his back to the dog. The dog opened its massive jaws and clamped down on the fur and flesh of Sho. Sho felt the sting. He had been wounded for the first time. Now he knew this creature must be killed. The two backed off and sized up each other for a minute. Then, at a distance of around twenty feet from one another, they ran and leapt into the air and met head on. As they met, Sho brushed aside the jaws of the beast with his left paw and then wrapped his jaws around the throat of the dog. Within sixty seconds the dog was dead, as its airway was completely shut off by the pressure Sho was exerting. Then Sho dragged the limp body of the dog over to the handlers. They were stunned. This trio had killed lions, tigers, bears and even people in the games in Rome. How had this lone dog killed these three? The handlers disappeared and a roar went up from all the people who had witnessed the event.

Jesus knew Sho had the protection of the Holy Spirit and the outcome was never in doubt. But still it was quite the feat from his best friend. Jesus simply smiled as he lovingly touched the open gash on Sho's back, and instantly the wound healed.

It was now clear to the members of the Sanhedrin getting rid of Jesus would not be an easy task. He had the massive crowds behind him and, of course,

Sho. Nothing, it seemed, could get past Jesus's guard dog. Perhaps there might be another way, Caiaphas thought to himself.

Now the Festival of Unleavened Bread, called the Passover, was approaching, and the chief priests and the teachers of the law were looking for some way to get rid of Jesus, for they were afraid of the people. Then Satan entered Judas, called Iscariot, one of the Twelve. And Judas went to the chief priests and the officers of the temple guard and discussed with them how he might betray Jesus. They were delighted and agreed to give him money. He consented, and watched for an opportunity to hand Jesus over to them when no crowd was present. (Luke 22:1-6)

Chapter 19

The Final Week

Tuesday and Wednesday

Jesus had set aside the entire day of Tuesday to teach and preach concerning a list of issues. His ultimate mission in teaching the people in the Temple was to show the way for his chosen disciples. He knew they would have to be the ones to carry forth the word. They must be shown and there wasn't much time left.

As Jesus and his "band" entered the Temple, the area was packed with pilgrims from across the land, both Gentiles and Jews. The Tuesday and Wednesday before Passover were always the busiest time of year in Jerusalem and the Temple. Sho immediately made a dash across the courtyard where he had dispatched the devil dogs a day earlier. There was no sign they were ever there except for several large blood stains still soaking in the pores of the stones that made up the patio. The Temple guards on duty stiffened with fear when Sho walked past them. Sho gave them little thought, however. Sho continued his patrol of the Temple grounds and all appeared to be safe for his Master and his disciples.

Every attempt by the Sanhedrin to rid Israel of Jesus had thus far failed. "Somehow we must get Rome to do the deed," Caiaphas said to the Sanhedrin. "Let's set a trap and get him to say something against Rome!"

They approached Jesus, who was in the middle of a sermon to a large group of people. *"Teacher, we know that you are honest, and don't defer to anyone; for you aren't partial to anyone, but truly teach the way of God. Is it lawful to pay taxes to Caesar, or not? Shall we give, or shall we not give?"*

But he, knowing their hypocrisy, said to them, **"Why do you test me? Bring me a denarius, that I may see it." They brought it. He said to them, "Whose is this image and inscription?"** They said to him, "Caesar's." Jesus answered them, **"Render to Caesar the things that are Caesar's, and to God the things that are God's."** They marveled greatly at him.

Jesus had smelled this trap immediately. They marveled not only at the wisdom of his answer, but that he had evaded their trap, once again! This happened on a Tuesday.

The next day, Wednesday, *Judas Iscariot, who was one of the twelve, went away to the chief priest, that he might deliver him to them. They, when they heard it, were glad, and promised to give him money.*

Now Caiaphas had what he wanted, someone from inside Jesus's band who would be willing to betray him. In turn Caiaphas offered Judas thirty pieces of silver. Judas jumped at the chance and began to plot against Jesus.

Jesus continued to teach to the crowds in Jerusalem that day to the point where there was no more room to handle the masses of people. The members of the Sanhedrin were in a panic because of the popularity of Jesus.

That evening, after returning to Bethany where Jesus was staying with friends, Jesus decided to take Sho for an evening walk. The disciples were very against this as they were worried about Jesus's safety, even with Sho by his side. Nevertheless Jesus and Sho disappeared into the darkness that evening walking toward the northwest. Sho was so very happy to be spending time alone with Jesus again. There had been only a handful of times the past three years when he and Jesus got to be alone. Sho was sick of all the crowds begging Jesus for this thing and that.

Finally, after walking a couple of miles, Jesus stopped at a clearing that had a small patch of soft grass. Jesus lay down, gazing up at the stars, and Sho joined him, resting his head on the chest of Jesus. The air was so clean and clear, the stars looked as though you could reach out and touch them. Sho loved sleeping with Jesus under the stars; he didn't much care for rooms in a house. Jesus enjoyed this as well. Jesus knew he would never have another night alone together with his best friend. They rolled in the grass together just as they had done years earlier when Jesus was a toddler and Sho a puppy. It was a beautiful sight seeing a man and his dog living in the moment.

Even God felt their love for one another at that moment and sensed that "this was good."

The day of unleavened bread came, on which the Passover must be sacrificed. He sent Peter and John saying, **"Go and prepare the Passover for us, that we may eat."** They said to him, "Where do you want us to prepare?"

He said to them, **"Behold, when you have entered into the city, a man carrying a pitcher of water will meet you. Follow him into the house which he enters. Tell the master of the house, 'The Teacher says to you, "Where is the guest room, where I may eat the Passover with my disciples?" He will show you a large, furnished upper room. Make preparation there."**

They went, found things as he had told them, and they prepared the Passover. When the hour had come, he sat down with the twelve apostles. He said to them, **"I have earnestly desired to eat this Passover with you before I suffer, for I tell you, I will no longer by any means eat of it until it is fulfilled in the Kingdom of God."** (Luke 22:7-16)

Chapter 20

The Final Week

Thursday

I t was now Thursday evening and Jesus was in an upper room where he had prearranged to have a last dinner with his chosen. He had purposely kept its whereabouts a secret for as long as possible as he did not want Judas knowing the location, lest he "turn him in". Jesus knew this would be his final time with his disciples. He knew this would be his "last supper" and wanted it to be a private, solemn moment for all.

Now, it had finally sunk into the minds of the twelve that Jesus was soon to die. They had heard Jesus make this proclamation time after time, but now that it was near they began to panic and think about their own situations. Insecurity crept into their minds.

Then Jesus said to them, *"All of you will be made to stumble because of me tonight, for it is written, 'I will strike the shepherd, and the sheep of the flock will be scattered.' But after I am raised up, I will go before you into Galilee."*

Peter, in an effort to combat everyone's insecurity (and his), blurted out, *"Even if all will be made to stumble because of you, I will never be made to stumble."* Jesus answered Peter and said, *"Most certainly I tell you that tonight, before the rooster crows, you will deny me three times."*

Peter sat down in shock that Jesus would say this of him. How could this be? he thought to himself. How could he ever deny his beloved Master?

After Peter sat down, Jesus said, *"Most certainly I tell you that one of you will betray me."* Now the group was in complete disarray. They all looked puzzled at one another. How could it be that one of the chosen could betray Jesus? Didn't we all love him? they asked.

He, leaning back, as he was, on Jesus's breast, asked him, "Lord, who is it?" Jesus therefore answered, *"It is he to whom I will give this piece of bread when I have dipped it."* So when he had dipped the piece of bread, he gave it to Judas, the *son of Simon Iscariot. After the piece of bread, then Satan entered into him.*

Then Jesus said to him, *"What you do, do quickly."*

Judas left the room and now there was but eleven. Sho was glad to see Judas leave. He never did smell right. Sho never trusted him and made certain he was never alone with Jesus. The others had no problem with Judas, only Sho. But God gave dogs the unique ability to judge the character of a human. It is a sixth sense humans do not have and dogs do. It cannot be explained away, only that it is real. Sho had his head on the lap of Jesus relaxing during the Passover meal. He had no interest in the wine being passed around, but Jesus did give him a piece of the sacred bread. This was enough for Sho, for at least his Master had taken the time to give him something.

During the meal Jesus did some final teachings and tried his best to prepare his remaining disciples for the difficult years to follow. *"If the world hates you, you know that it has hated me before it hated you. If you were of the world, the world would love its own. But because you are not of the world, since I chose you out of the world, therefore the world hates you."* Then Jesus went on to follow, *"These things have I spoken to you, so that you wouldn't be*

caused to stumble. They will put you out of the syn-
agogues. Yes, the time come that whoever kills you
will think that he offers service to God. They will
do these things because they have not known the
Father, nor me. But I have told you these things, so
that when the time comes you may remember that I
told you about them."

Now it was official; they were all going to die for
the cause of Jesus and Jesus let them know.

After their Final Supper together, they left the
upper room and went to a place called Gethsemane,
which was not far outside of Jerusalem. This was a
favorite spot for Jesus while in Jerusalem, as it had a
large garden area with many olive trees, some as old
as five hundred years.

Jesus had his disciples sit in an area and prayed
while he took Peter, James and John with him to the
far end of the garden area. Jesus immediately began
praying that his Father, God, would not have him
die on the cross. For the first time in his life Jesus
prayed for himself, not wanting to die and prayed,
"My Father, if this cup can't pass away from me
unless I drink it, your desire be done." Then it was
revealed to Jesus that he must die for the sins of man
and he accepted his fate.

Then, looking around, he saw all the disciples asleep as it had been a very, very long day and week and they simply could not stay awake. Even Sho was hard asleep. Then Jesus made a final and surprising prayer. Looking upward to heaven he asked, **"Father I ask one more thing of you. I know Sho will never let come to pass what must come to pass, so I ask you take away the protection of the Holy Spirit from him."**

With that Jesus looked down at the sleeping Sho and instantly the same light orb that had landed on Jesus the day of his baptism on the Jordan River, the same orb Sho had chased through the desert that night, exited the body of Sho and slowly drifted away through the garden toward the heavens. Jesus began weeping over the sleeping body of his best friend, for he knew what it meant. Jesus knew it was soon to be the end for the both of them. Sho awoke suddenly and was immediately alarmed to see Jesus was crying. He looked around and it appeared all was allright, so he began licking the tears away from the face of Jesus. He wondered why Jesus was crying. Then Jesus picked him up and carried him back to where the disciples were sleeping. He awoke them and, holding Sho in his muscular arms, said the following, **"Without this creature God gave** me at birth, I could not have fulfilled my mission with you. Sho taught me the meaning of love. Not just any love, but the purest of love—total unconditional love. This lesson I have tried to pass on to you and all men. He saved my life too many times to count. But most of all he was my friend, my only real friend on this world. So I say this forevermore to be recorded, that a dog is man's best friend." And from that time on, passed down through the ages, began the saying "man's best friend" in reference to a dog.

With that said he gave Sho the biggest embrace of his life and gently put him on the ground. Sho didn't know what Jesus had said, but he could sense something different with Jesus. Sho didn't know whether to be happy or sad, just that Jesus's emotions were flowing like a strong river. The disciples didn't quite know what to make of this either.

Just as Jesus had finished saying this, Judas arrived with a group of Temple guards who were armed with swords and clubs. They were sent by the chief priests and the entire Sanhedrin to arrest Jesus. Judas had arranged a signal to the guards ahead of time, that the man he approached and gave a kiss to would be Jesus. As he approached Jesus, Sho let out a loud growl and this really scared Judas, as he knew what Sho was capable of. He quickly kissed Jesus and backed off. Then Jesus said to him, *"Judas, do you betray the Son of Man with a kiss?"* Then the guards tried to seize Jesus. Jesus did not resist, but two things happened simultaneously.

Peter drew his sword and struck the servant of the high priest, cutting off his ear. Jesus quickly picked the ear off the ground and placed it back on the man's head, completely healed.

At the same instant Sho leapt into action the moment the guards surrounded Jesus to take him away. He was ready to kill each and every one of them. But as he was airborne and ready to dispatch his first victim, he felt the blunt force of a wooden club knocking him to the ground.

As Sho looked up, Jesus was being led away and all of his disciples had fled and deserted him. Sho couldn't understand as he did not have the strength to get up and fight back his tormentors. Then a half dozen Temple guards, including the three handlers of Pilate's death dogs, proceeded to beat Sho to the point of death. Had God and Jesus abandoned him? he thought as blow after blow brought him closer to death.

Overhead in the garden was a legion of angels with razor-sharp swords clamoring to come to Sho's rescue—but God would not allow it.

After repeated blows to his head and body, the guards figured Sho to be dead. In a final act of savagery, one of the guards took his sword out and cut off the right front paw of Sho. Then another stuck his sword into his right eye and this left his eyeball hanging from its socket. The men hurried to catch up with the group that had captured Jesus. They wanted to be seen as returning with the prize to the Sanhedrin for Caiaphas had offered a bounty of thirty pieces of silver for anyone who could prove they had killed the mighty Shomer.

They escorted Jesus to Caiaphas and the high priests, then one of guards tossed the severed paw of Sho at the feet of Caiaphas. For the first time in his life, as Jesus was staring at the severed foot of his best friend, he experienced the emotion of rage and revenge! For several seconds Jesus considered calling his mission on Earth to a halt, grabbing a sword and call on the angels of Heaven to cleanse the Temple! He was so enraged someone could hurt his precious Sho like this, he began to sweat droplets of blood. Then just in time, the Holy Spirit that had left Sho descended on Jesus and a wonderful calm and peace enveloped him. Jesus was now back on track to complete his mission.

Jesus would now go on trial for his life. It was telling that this group of Jews was doing all this under the cover of darkness, for they knew how the people loved Jesus and his arrest would cause riots in the streets of Jerusalem. For several hours the priests interrogated Jesus, trying to get him to incriminate himself as they could not get enough witnesses to agree as to his alleged blasphemy. Finally, as the night was drawing to an end and the sun soon to rise, the high priest asked Jesus, *"Are you the Christ, the Son of God?"*

"I am," said Jesus, *"And you will see the Son of Man sitting at the right hand of the Mighty One and coming on the clouds of heaven."*

That sealed the fate of Jesus and all the priests condemned him to death. Some began to spit on him in contempt. Then they blindfolded him and struck him with their fists. Then the guards beat him without mercy.

While Peter was below in the courtyard, one of the servant girls of the high priest came by. When she saw Peter warming himself, she looked closely at him. 'You also were with that Nazarene, Jesus,' she said. But he denied it. 'I don't know or understand what you're talking about,' he said, and went out into the entryway. When the servant girl saw him there, she said again to those standing around, 'This fellow is one of them.' Again he denied it. After a little while, those standing near said to Peter, 'Surely you are one of them, for you are a Galilean.'

He began to call down curses on himself, and swore to them, 'I don't know this man you're talking about.' Immediately the rooster crowed the second time. Then Peter remembered the word Jesus had spoken to him: 'Before the rooster crows twice you will disown me three times.' And he broke down and wept."

Immediately in the morning the chief priests, with the elders and scribes, and the whole council held a consultation, and bound Jesus, and carried him away, and delivered him up to Pilate. Pilate asked him, "Are you the King of the Jews?"

*He answered, **"So you say."***

The chief priests accused him of many things. Pilate again asked him, "Have you no answer? See how many things they testify against you!"

But Jesus made no further answer, so that Pilate marveled. (Mark 15:1-5)

Chapter 21

Friday: The Final Day

Pilate was at a crossroads. As far as Rome was concerned, Jesus was but a joke and posed no threat to the Empire. He had no army. His followers had no political slogans. He was told by a spy about the incident at the Temple where Jesus told the Jews who were trying to trap him to "render unto Caesar the things that were Caesar's and unto God the things that were God's." This, Pilate thought, was not a person Rome need worry about.

Still, it was obvious to Pilate the ruling religious elites of the country wanted this man out of their way. Jesus was a clear threat to their world order and they wanted him dead and now they wanted Rome to do the dirty work as Jesus was just too popular with the masses.

As the sun rose in the east on that Friday morning, it would be the beginning of the most important day in human history. It was the custom during Passover to release a prisoner who the people requested. There was a man named Barabbas who was a Zealot. The Zealots were a radical political group whose ultimate aim was to drive Rome out of Israel. Barabbas had recently killed someone in a skirmish and was awaiting death. So on that Friday morning Pilate addressed the crowd from a place high above the mob and offered them the choice of Jesus or Barabbas. At first there was silence. Then to the surprise of Pilate, the crowd began chanting the name of Barabbas. They wanted the release of Barabbas instead of Jesus? Pilate was dumbfounded. There were some in the crowd shouting out the name of Jesus, but the people calling out the name of Barabbas far outnumbered those of Jesus's supporters.

How could this be? Pilate thought. Only a few days ago all of Jerusalem was greeting the "prophet" at his entry into Jerusalem. Not known to Pilate, however, the Sanhedrin was taking no chances and emptied the Temple treasury offering pieces of silver to anyone who would shout out to have Barabbas saved. The people loved Jesus, but for money Caiaphas knew they would turn on him.

Jesus was listening to this and recalled the name Barabbas. He was the person when they were children who attacked him after school. He was the boy Sho had almost killed. Now, in a strange twist of history, Jesus was going to exchange his life for that of Barabbas. After the mob insisted Barabbas be exchanged for Jesus, Pilate ordered Barabbas released and directed Jesus be flogged and then crucified.

On the other side of Jerusalem, at the Garden, Sho had finally risen from his beating. He noticed his vision was blurred and he could not see out of his right eye. He could feel something hanging where his eye used to be, but did not know what it was. As he tried to get up he stumbled several times and had a difficult time of balancing himself. Then he looked down and noticed his right front paw was missing. His right leg was little more than a stub. He crawled over to the nearest olive tree to use it for balance and managed to get up on his three remaining legs. He badly needed water. He lifted his nose into the wind and could smell water down the hillside. That would be the brook of Kidron. He knew it well, as Jesus used this as a water source many times. Somehow, between crawling and rolling, he managed to reach the edge of the creek. After soaking his amputated leg in the cool stream and refreshing himself with all the water he could hold, he set out to find Jesus.

He was in terrible pain, but the pain of not having Jesus near him overrode any feelings he had toward his own body. He would find Jesus if it killed him, he thought.

Once he made his way within the gates of Jerusalem he immediately got scent of Jesus. His legs were now useless, his remarkable eyesight was gone, he had lost his powers, but he still had his ultra-keen sense of hearing and smell. The scent led him to the palace used by Roman officials when they were in Jerusalem.

As he hobbled through the streets of Jerusalem, no one recognized him any longer. He was so bloodied his white fur was barely distinguishable. With his eye dangling from its socket and hobbling on three legs, no one could tell this was the mighty Shomer. No one would approach the pathetic-looking dog to offer help.

As he was making his way across Jerusalem to the prison where they were holding Jesus, he came across the body of Judas hanging from a rope. He gazed up with his one good eye at his body dangling like a leaf in the wind and let out a loud growl. He was the one who had started all this when he walked up to Jesus and betrayed him. Sho was content to see Judas dead. He never trusted that man as he never did smell right. Now the vultures were circling overhead to feast off the lowest of all men.

The Roman guards led Jesus away into an open courtyard in the palace where they flogged the enemies of Rome. In the middle of the yard was a massive wooden post well secured into the ground. Many men had suffered at this spot. They tied Jesus and stripped him of his clothes. Jesus was now about to experience the most feared thing in all of the ancient world—the cat of nine tails. This was a whip with nine tapered leather straps that all came to a sharp point at the end. Bound with a three-foot-long piece of wood, its effects when landing on human flesh were devastating. Each time the whip landed, it was the equivalent of nine separate whips slicing through skin. Jesus was ordered thirty- nine lashes from the cat of nine tails. The guard with most seniority took the whip and drew back with all his might. He had done this to many men before. His first mark sliced nine cuts on the back of Jesus and blood gushed everywhere. One down, thirty eight to go. Two. Three. Four. Five. Jesus braced himself as he could hear the whip cut through the air before landing on his back. Six. Seven. Eight. Nine. Blood was pouring down the back of Jesus. Ten. Eleven. Twelve. Thirteen. Fourteen. Fifteen. Sixteen. The guard then paused and asked for some water. Some thought he would be compassionate and offer Jesus some relief with the water, but the guard drank it himself. Then he resumed. Seventeen. Eighteen. Nineteen. Twenty. Twenty-one. Twenty-two. Twenty-three. Twenty-four. Twenty-five. Then on the twenty-sixth blow one of leather points dug deep into the back of Jesus and blood shot out in a stream, striking the guard in the eyes, and he immediately went blind. Jesus, after twenty six blows was barely hanging onto life. The guard was screaming because of his blindness, while Jesus never let out a sound. How could this be? onlookers thought. Jesus would not let Rome, or the Sanhedrin, or Satan have the satisfaction of knowing how deep was his pain.

Then another guard quickly picked up the whip, drew back with all his might, and landed the cat on its mark once again. Twenty-seven. Twenty-eight. Twenty-nine. Thirty. Thirty-one. Thirty-two. Thirty-three. Thirty-four. Thirty-five. Thirty-six. Thirty-seven. Thirty-eight. Finally, thirty-nine. A strange figure, clothed in black, with dark features more animal like than human, stood in the corner of the yard and had a grisly smile on its face. Satan was enjoying the show put on by the Romans.

From behind, Jesus didn't even look human. His back was a ribbon of torn flesh and blood. As they cut him down from the post, he collapsed on the ground and crawled over to the guard who had become blinded by Jesus's blood. He reached out with the little remaining strength he had and touched the eyes of the man and immediately he could see again. The whip master asked Jesus to forgive him and Jesus said, **"You are forgiven for what you have done."** Returning the sight of the Roman commander was the last miracle Jesus would ever perform. The next day, as the commander returned to the place of the beating, he noticed large patches of Easter lilies at the base of the post where Jesus had been bound and beaten. It looked as though wherever his blood had touched the ground a lily had sprung up overnight.

Then the governor's soldiers took Jesus into the Praetorium and gathered the whole garrison together against him. They stripped and put a scarlet robe on him. They braided a crown of thorns and put it on his head and a reed in his right hand; and they kneeled down before him, and mocked him, saying, "Hail, King of the Jews!" They spat on him, and took the reed and struck him on the head. When they had mocked him, they took the robe off of him, and put his clothes on him, and led him away to crucify him.

By the time he could get to Jesus he was stretched out on a cross. Sho, no longer able to hobble, crawled the remaining fifty feet up the hill. He passed by Mary and Mary Magdalene and John. Mary was in tears and when she saw Sho crawling toward the foot of the cross, she fainted. Mary Magdalene and John slowly revived Mary and she was shaking fiercely. Seeing her son stretched out on a cross, the most horrible of all deaths, was too much for her to bear. Then to see Sho, with only one front leg, bloodied and his right eye dangling from its socket was overwhelming. Mary had always thought of Sho as a family member, as close to her as her children… and her mind went back to that evening over thirty years ago in Bethlehem when she held Jesus in her arms and looked down at her feet and there was Shomer no bigger than her hand. This brought a brief smile to her face and she was able to breathe again.

Jesus was now hanging on the wooden cross, clinging onto life by a thread. Rome was outdoing itself this Passover as it had also condemned two others to die by crucifixion. Jesus was heard to say to God*, "Father forgive them, for they do not know what they are doing." And they divided up his clothes by casting lots. The soldiers also came up* *and mocked him. They offered him wine vinegar and said, "If you are the king of the Jews, save yourself."*

Sho was at the foot of the cross now and unable to do anything to help his friend and Master. Several of the guards surrounded Sho and kicked him away from the cross. As he rolled down the hill, he wanted nothing more than to rip open the throats of these men, but his body would not respond. All he could do was gaze up at his best friend and utter a desperate moan because of his inability to help Jesus.

Then one of the criminals who hung next to Jesus hurled insults at him saying, *"If you are the Christ, save yourself and us!" But the other answered, and rebuked him said, "Don't you fear God, seeing you are under the same condemnation? And we indeed justly, for we receive the due reward for our deeds, but this man has done nothing wrong." He said to Jesus, "Lord, remember me when you come into your Kingdom".*

Jesus said to him, **"Assuredly I tell you, today you will be with me in Paradise."** And he looked down upon his precious Sho and seeing the terrible things they had done to him… Jesus called out with a loud breath, **"Father, into your hands I commit my spirit!"** Having said this, he breathed his last.

Mary, John, Mary Magdalene and others who loved Jesus burst out into wailing. The only perfect human who ever lived had been rejected and brutally killed and it was all too much to bear. Even the earth was in turmoil as the sky went dark and a tremendous earthquake rumbled throughout Jerusalem as if to say, "Today you have killed God's son."

Then the mighty Shomer summoned his last ounce of strength and managed to crawl up to the foot of his Master's cross. With his last drop of energy, he dug his hind legs into the ground, and leaning on the cross, propped himself up and took the deepest breath of his life, letting out a blood-curdling howl that could be heard across Jerusalem, echoing through the palace and Temple walls and the streets of Jerusalem. Then, as the last bit of air left his lungs, the mighty Sho collapsed and his spirit left his body, joining Jesus once again. They had been separated only by a couple of minutes.

John, the beloved disciple who was present, said, he died from a "broken heart." And this is where and when this saying originated. Sho's heart had burst open when he knew his Master had died. Jesus had given his life in exchange for that of the human race and Sho had given his life to protect the One who was charged with that task. Together they gave their lives for that one cause.

When evening had come, a rich man from Arimathaea, named Joseph, who himself was also Jesus's disciple came.

This man went to Pilate, and asked for Jesus's body. Then Pilate commanded the body to be given up. Joseph took the body, and wrapped it in a clean linen cloth, and laid it in his own new tomb, which he had hewn out in the rock, and he rolled a great stone to the door of the tomb, and departed. Mary Magdalene was there, and the other Mary, sitting opposite the tomb. (Matthew 27:57-61)

Chapter 22

Burial and Resurrection

Mary was in no condition to deal with burial plans for her son, so she relied on John to oversee the details. Mary was heartbroken and still in shock as she tried to weave together the extraordinary events of her life and those of Jesus. From that magical night in the stable in Bethlehem over thirty years ago, she had always wondered about the true meaning of her giving birth as a virgin, the many strange things that happened while raising Jesus and her occasional visits from angels. These thoughts were now racing through her mind as she gazed upon the limp body of her beloved son.

Mary made only one decision for the burial of Jesus and the rest she turned over to John and James. She insisted Sho be buried with Jesus. She knew Jesus would want this. No one had ever had a dog entombed with them in all the centuries of Jewish life. But no dog was ever like Sho, Mary thought. It would only be fitting they be buried together. They were born together and they should be buried together.

Then Joseph, John and James carefully carried the body of Jesus and laid him in a tomb Joseph of Arimathea had carved out of a hillside on the outskirts of Jerusalem. They did the same for Shomer. John was weeping as they wrapped the broken, bloodied bodies of both Jesus and Sho. John remembered back in time when he first met Jesus, standing tall and confident in his every action and thought along the shore of the Sea of Galilee. Then there was Sho sitting at the right side of Jesus, confident in his every action and thought. Together they were beyond impressive. They were two, but thought and operated and loved each other as one. He remembered the event like it was yesterday as the dog broke from the side of Jesus and ran up to him, gently taking his hand in his huge mouth and leading him to Jesus. That was how it started for John. How could it all end like this? John thought to himself.

They laid the beaten, broken body of Jesus on a sandstone slab, and at the insistence of Mary, they also took the broken body of Sho and laid him at the foot of Jesus. The silence within the tomb was deafening and the only sound you could hear were the wails of Jesus's supporters and loved ones outside the tomb.

Mary then somehow managed the strength to enter the tomb. Slowly she made her way to Jesus and gave him a final kiss on his bloodied forehead, where the deep cuts from the crown of thorns had dug into his skin. Then in a surprise to all, she bent over and pulled the burial cloth away from the battered body of Sho and gave him a similar kiss on his forehead. Then she pulled an object out of her pocket and gingerly placed a wooden toy Jesus had carved as a young boy for Sho upon his chest and pulled the burial linen back over his body. The wooden toy resembled a crocodile and it was the first thing Jesus carved as a boy as he was learning to use the carpenter's knife.

As she made her exit from the tomb she could hear in her mind the bark of a playful dog and the laugh of a young boy many years ago playing along the banks of the Nile. Again she fainted and collapsed to the ground, her fall broken at the last second as Mary M. was able to cushion the fall by grabbing onto her shoulders.

Then, just as the sun was setting in the West, six-able bodied men surrounded the large hand carved stone meant to seal the tomb forever. After several attempts they finally rolled the stone into a permanent notched position meant to lock the tomb forever.

The next day all the disciples were in disarray and shock. They had all fled and scattered when Jesus was confronted by the Temple authorities. They might have stayed and fought off the guards, but when they had seen that Sho was no longer able to protect them and was getting savagely beaten, they had decided to flee. Now the guilt each felt was worse than death itself. At the time when it meant the most, they buckled and left Jesus to the Romans. In many ways they were guiltier than the Romans, for Jesus said, *"God forgive them for they know not what they are doing."* The disciples, however, did know better—hence the guilt. The Romans felt no guilt—to them Jesus was just another man. The disciples knew better.

So all day that day, Saturday, the disciples languished in shock and dismay over the events that not only occurred that week but over the previous three years. Each of the disciples relived in their minds special times they had with Jesus. All the private conversations he had with each. They were now a group of men without a leader—or so they thought.

When the Sabbath was past, Mary Magdalene and Mary the mother of James and Salome, bought spices, that they might come and anoint him. Very early on the first day of the week, they came to the tomb when the sun had risen. They were saying among themselves, "Who will roll away the stone from the door of the tomb for us?" for it was very big. Looking up, they saw that the stone was rolled back.

Entering into the tomb, they saw a young man sitting on the right side, dressed in a white robe, and they were amazed. He said to them, "Don't be amazed. You seek Jesus, the Nazarene, who has been crucified. He has risen. He is not here. Behold, the place where they laid him!"

"But go, tell his disciples and Peter, 'He goes before you into Galilee. There you will see him, as he said to you.'"

Inside the tomb was the empty shroud of Jesus lying on the sandstone slab. At the base of the slab was the empty shroud of Sho. The only other item in the tomb was the chewed-up wooden toy Jesus had carved for Sho as a boy. And that is the story of the birth, youth, life, ministry, death and resurrection of Jesus and his "best friend"—Shomer.

Truly the greatest love story ever told about a man and a dog!

Epilogue

T hen I awoke from the dream, in a cold sweat, wondering, was this all a dream or an actual visitation? And the first thing I saw after awakening was my seventy pound dog, Cabo, licking my face, worried about my condition. Then I deliberately stared into his large brown eyes, hoping to see a little bit of Sho in him and I knew immediately HE would have the faith to walk over water, but would I?

Won't You Lend Us A Paw?

I n today's world of publishing, self-publishing, which is the method I choose for this book, has now become very commonplace. It has pluses and minuses, but basically it means that all marketing for the book is left up to the author. Since I don't have a big budget to spend on the book for marketing I'd *like* to *rely* on *you* to help out and spread the word about this book. People telling people is the best advertising in the world.

If you feel this book has value to you and, therefore to others, won't you consider going out of your way to recommend it or my website to twelve likeminded people? These would typically be people who are animal lovers of all sorts, your Christian friends, coworkers, vet, groomer, social media con-tacts-just about anyone. But especially get this book in the hands of young people!

Jesus changed the world by commissioning twelve people to spread the word.

I'd like to commission you to telling twelve people about this book.

For those who choose not to share this story, but would like to *donate* copies of this book to institutions like schools, libraries, churches or animal shelters for fundraising, etc., please refer to my website, as it has contact information.

May God bless you and don't forget to take your dog on a wonderful walk today and open your Bible as well.

Useful Links

www.ebible.org

The World English Bible is a Public Domain (no copyright) Modern English translation of the Holy Bible. Most bible citations in this book are from the WEB.

www.bestfriends.org

These are wonderful people that have *no* other agenda than the welfare of animals. If you are looking to help support a "no kill" animal shelter, you can't go wrong with them.

www.k9deli.net

<u>If you might be looking to upgrade the quality of your pet's food you should check this out.</u> This is the only food we personally feed our pets. The products are all-natural, human grade ingredients, always fresh and delivered right to your door. There is also a

wonderful home-based business opportunity with the company if you are so inclined.

www.ifJesushadadog.com

This is my personal website and has contact information. Note: the book in now available in audio book.